Darwin's Submarine I-124

Tom Lewis

To Ron & Pat once more

Published by Avonmore Books

PO Box 217, Kent Town South Australia 5071 Australia

www.avonmorebooks.com.au

Printed by Everbest, China

Graphic design by Diane Bricknell, Swansea, Tasmania

Inside front/back covers & back cover painting by Bob McRae, War artist, Wollongong, NSW, Australia

ISBN: 978 0 957 73519 4

Cataloguing in publication information supplied by the Northern Territory Library:

Lewis, Tom, 1958-

Darwin's Submarine *I-124*. Kent Town South Australia: Avonmore Books, 2010.

ISBN: 0 646 32218 4

1. Submarine boats - Northern Territory.

2. Submarine Warfare - Northern Territory

3. Shipwrecks - Northern Territory - Clarence Strait.

4. World war, 1939-1945 - Northern Territory - Naval operations - Submarine

5. Salvage - Northern Territory - Clarence Strait.

I. Title

940.5451

Note to this edition. The main content of this work was published in 1997 under the title of *Sensuikan I-124* with an ISBN of 0 646 32218 4. This work, in B5 format as opposed to A4, carries many more graphics and improvements and additions to the text.

Contents

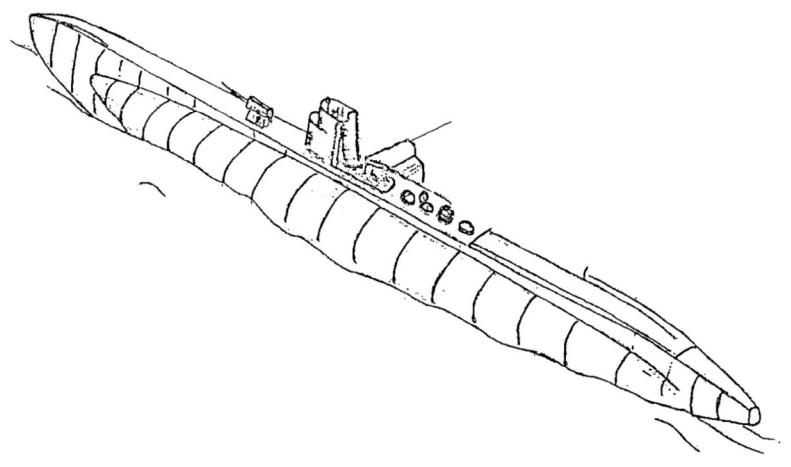

Foreword

BY HIS HONOUR AUSTIN ASCHE AC, QC

The spectacular success of the Japanese air raids on Darwin on 19th February 1942 has tended to obscure the fact that an equally dangerous threat to shipping entering or leaving Darwin harbour was posed by the submarines of the Imperial Japanese Navy lurking outside. Contemporary records exist of this very real threat, and the subject has not gone wholly unnoticed by historians and commentators, both Japanese and Australian. But it has been left to Dr Lewis to gather together these various sources, and present us with a competent and carefully researched account of an episode which, while certainly not as dramatic as the destruction of Darwin from the sky, still carried its own special danger and menace from the sea; which, happily, was averted by an efficient and successful attack by Australian and American ships.

The four Japanese submarines positioned outside Darwin harbour as early as January 1942 were certainly capable of causing great damage to any ships in the vicinity. Dr Lewis carefully describes their equipment and armour, and their potential for aggressive action against Allied shipping. The submarines were equipped with both mines and torpedos. Their crews were efficient and their leaders highly so. Dr Lewis describes vividly the rigorous course of training undertaken by those officers of the Japanese Navy who aspired to this branch of the Service, and the high prestige attached to it. This was a dangerous foe. It was met by equally determined defenders.

The book proceeds with a vivid and exciting account of the manoeuvres of the Allied ships from the first observed torpedo attack (a narrow miss), to the final destruction of the submarine *I-124*. Dr Lewis here successfully achieves a rather difficult task; insofar as he manages to describe the technical details of these encounters sufficiently to satisfy the expert, but still gives amateurs, (such as myself), a clear understanding of the basic situation. His account clearly sets out the actions of all ships concerned and very carefully describes the individual contribution of each. Various earlier versions are examined and discarded as not reliable as against the body of proven fact.

The result is that, without in any way denigrating the efforts of others, the ultimate recognition and credit for the destruction of the submarine must go to the crew of *HMAS Deloraine* under the command of the highly competent Lieutenant Commander Desmond Menlove; and we are given the family background and naval training of this fine Australian, which enabled him to figure with distinction on the day, and go on to further conspicuous service for his country. For good measure and to render the story complete, the professional and family backgrounds of Lieutenant Commander Kishigami of Submarine *I-124* and Commander Endo, the Squadron Commander, are given in such a way as to remind us of their status as human beings and family men, rather than the evil fanatics which most Australians would have thought them at the time.

The sinking of the *I-124* and the dispersal of the other three submarines in the squadron outside Darwin Harbour was one ray of light in an otherwise dark beginning to 1942. Furthermore, it establishes that, as far as sea defence was concerned, Darwin was not entirely unprepared. Dr Lewis reminds us that,

> … a massive harbour boom was built across the entrance to the harbour. This was a floating fence, extending several miles, and by far the largest in Australia. … By late January 1942 two vessels were serving as permanent gate vessels, three others were in service maintaining the boom itself (and) … for defence against mines the 70th Auxiliary Mine Sweeper Squadron, consisting of a couple of converted civilian coasters (later three), maintained a swept channel into the harbour entrance.

This does indicate that someone, somehow, somewhere, before the attack on Darwin, had given some forethought to its defence. In the broad spectrum it may seem hopelessly inadequate, but it is fair to remember its existence in the general condemnation of the authorities of the time. Vast amounts of paper have been expended by subsequent commentators deploring the blindness, the inaction, the failure to comprehend obvious dangers; and, indeed, the positive stupidity of many of those then in charge of our defences; and it would be fruitless to deny that glaring mistakes did not occur. But, inevitably, a democracy is slower to react to perceived threats, because the people must be informed and persuaded that such threats exist. One can point to much the same ignorance, confusion and shock existing in Britain before Dunkirk, and in the USA before Pearl Harbour. A dictatorship or autocracy, such as Germany and Japan then were, has the advantage of immediate action because the leaders simply give the orders and the people obey.

Furthermore, positive movements were even then taking place to strengthen Darwin's defences, and, given a few more months, Darwin may have been much better equipped. What frustrated these preparations was time. The speed of the Japanese advance was extraordinary, and, according to some authorities, took even the Japanese by surprise.

Dr Lewis also gives us some comfort in another direction. The apparently ruthlessly efficient enemy was just as capable of making mistakes as the Allies. In particular, they employed their considerable submarine strength in a highly inefficient manner.

Rather than using the (submarine) fleet for pursuing one aim, as the U-boats were used in the wolf-pack tactics that nearly won for Germany the Battle of the Atlantic, for example, the Japanese submarine fleet was employed on a variety of interesting but highly ineffective tasks, ranging from deploying seaplanes, midget submarines...to acting as seaplane refuelers and underwater transports, they could have made a significant alteration to the results of the war if they had been handled effectively.

To confirm his own observation as given above, Dr Lewis cites a similar view by a Japanese historian: "In spite of the size, spirit and reputation, this redoubtable force proved to be an almost total failure."

Having given us, in dramatic detail, the story of the pursuit and defeat of the Japanese submarines outside Darwin Harbour, Dr Lewis then turns his attention to the correction and deflating of a number of fascinating urban myths which have somehow attached themselves to the sunken submarine *I-124*. He does this with great care and fairness, meticulously tracing their origins, and establishing, by detailed research, that they are false, or, at most, wildly improbable. There was gold on board, there were large amounts of mercury, (poisoning the fish), there was another sunken submarine nearby, the crew had been heard tapping inside the craft, and, apparently, in some mysterious way, the submarine had been involved in the sinking of *HMAS Sydney* at the other end of the continent.

No doubt some of these myths arose from rival claims to salvage the vessel, and Dr Lewis introduces us to some colourful characters. But, while some of the plans to salvage were for profit, there were equally claims for sentiment. The elder daughter of Lieutenant Commander Kishigami sought, for many years, the return of her father's remains for a traditional Japanese burial, and gained support from many Japanese people, touched by the story of a loyal daughter and the memory of old and revered customs. Salvage now appears unlikely since the decision of both Australian and Japanese Governments is that the vessel should stay unviolated; as an approved War Grave respected by both nations.

This book has been painstakingly researched, and convincingly related in both strategic and human terms. It tells of an early incident in the exploits of the RAN in the Pacific War which reflects great credit on the Service, and should be better known; and now, I trust, will be.

Austin Asche

The Honourable Austin Asche AC, QC is a former Administrator of the Northern Territory

EXPLANATORY NOTES

Tonnages of ships and their measurements are given as quoted in original figures; as are verbatim accounts of distance and speed;

The 24 hour military system of time is used when describing the movements and operations of naval vessels during World War II. Thus 8am is 0800, 12 noon 1200 hours, and then the time becomes 1300 hours for 1pm; 6.15 pm is 1815 and so on.

Sections of Chapter One were written originally for an essay – "The Navy in Darwin in World War II" – which won the Kath Manzie History Award, a section of the NT Literary Awards. The essay was subsequently published in *Australia's Navy - 1995*, Canberra: Department of Defence, 1995. Various compilations of the book have been published in magazines and periodicals since the first edition's publication.

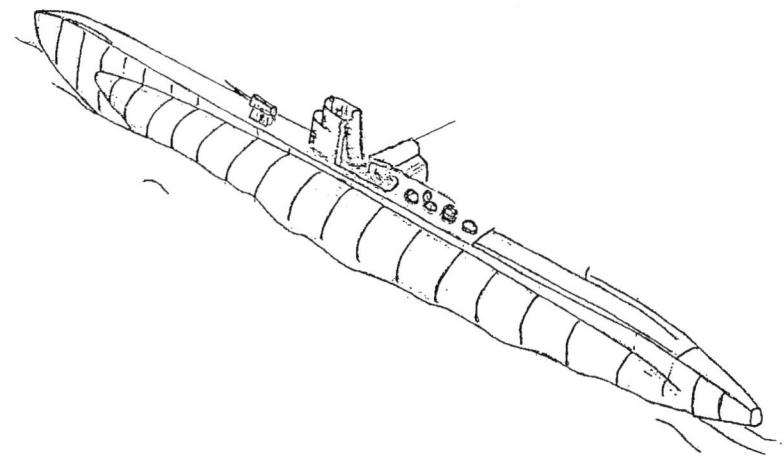

ACKNOWLEDGEMENTS

Thanks for their assistance in completing this publication are expressed to the following:

Northern Territory Government, whose NT History Awards sponsored initial research in Japan;

Librarians Michael Loos, David Swift; aviation expert and historian;

Don Kibbler, founder of the Cowra War Gardens, for initial assistance in Japanese research; Jeff Maynard, and his film *Niagara's Gold*;

In Japan: Captain (ret.) Teruaki Kawano, of the National Institute for Defence Studies, Tokyo; Atsuko Kishigami, whose hospitality and honesty made a very long journey so worthwhile; Ken Yonemoto, for escorts to interviews and locations; Simon and Hiromi Loveday;

HMAS Deloraine member Frank Marsh;

Naval personnel Greg Swinden, Peter Siebert, Brett Dowsing, Ian Gibson, Steve Cole, Andrew MacKinnon, Ian Watts;

Commentators Margie Cole, Keith Moylan, Terry Foster; Terry Connors; Jim Porter; Neil Molloy; Michelle Breen; Tom Dinning; Glen Smith; Kelly Moylan; Kaylene Anderson, Paul Maher; and Ron and Pat Lewis.

Historians John Bradford, Peter Williams, Iris Nesdale, David Stevens, Mike McCarthy, Alan Powell, Bob Alford; *HMAS Warrnambool* member and author of *The Secret Battle* Bob Wallace, for technical advice;

Scuba divers Phil Franklin, Steve Cole; Sasha Muller, Suzie Lack;

RAAF Group Captain Peter McDermott;

Graphic artists Jennifer Croxford, Diane Bricknell, Peter Ingman and War artist Bob McRae, and translators Simon Loveday, Jodie Kell and Li Xiao.

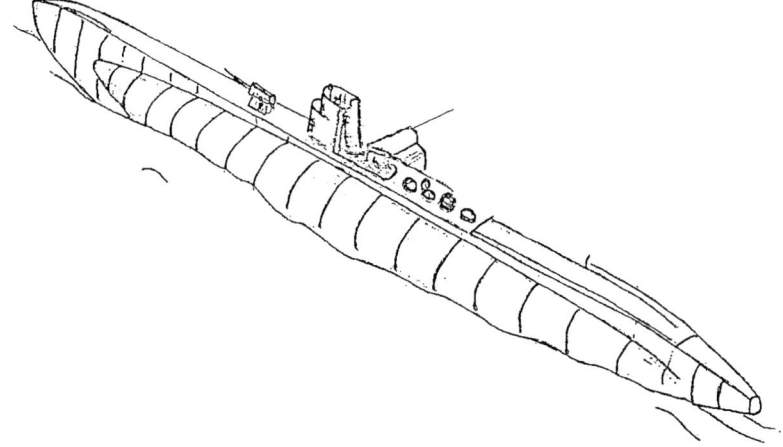

CHAPTER ONE

– A SUBMARINE'S STORY IN WAR AND PEACE

The Imperial Japanese Navy fleet submarine *I-124* was the first Japanese submarine sunk by the Royal Australian Navy in World War II. It lies complete outside the modern port of Darwin, Australia's northernmost city. Containing the bodies of 80 members of the once-proud mighty Japanese fleet, it bears no pride of place on the walls of Japanese museums. Its 80 men's names are not celebrated or remembered on any memorial – this book is the only listing made, so far, of those four-score brave warriors.

Despite that, the *I-124* has many other mysteries surrounding her. She was one of the first Japanese submarines to sink Allied ships in WWII. It is still claimed in several books that she held secret codes that were recovered by American divers, thus providing an invaluable aid to the Allied victory. She has been the subject of suggestions that her hull holds secrets about *HMAS Sydney*, the valiant light cruiser which fought bravely off the Western Australian coast in 1941, but which was sunk by the German raider *Kormoran*.

Post-war the *I-124* was the subject of salvage claims during the 1970s that led to bitter division between the competing recovery crews, whose vulgar fighting led to the Australian Historic Shipwrecks Act which still protects the submarine wreck today. In modern times *I-124* was said to be holding a valuable ballast of mercury, the leaking of which into the surrounding seas was causing fish poisoning.

Darwin's Submarine I-124 also gives an insight into the proud story of her conqueror, the corvette *HMAS Deloraine*. The attack by the submarine and her three sister boats was also the opening pages of a campaign against Darwin's ability to mount attacks against the oncoming and all-successful Japanese in what were extremely dark days for the comparatively new nation of Australia. The submarine attack, it will be shown, failed utterly, and almost a month to the day, on 19 February 1942, the Mobile Force of the IJN approached Australia, and this time there was no mistake. They mounted the most successful strike ever made against Australian soil, killing hundreds; sinking ships and downing aircraft. The book therefore is the oft-forgotten chapter of what some have called the "Battle for Australia".

This is the story of perhaps the most exciting and interesting shipwreck in Australian waters.

A peaceful Darwin waterfront in 1940. On the left is the angled pier, which made loading ships even more difficult than the huge tides dictated. Loads were awkwardly moved around the bend via a railway turntable. The port's large oil tanks dominate the foreground, while to the right can be seen Fort Hill, later demolished. Over the next five years the port grew enormously: on 19 February 1942, when the Japanese attacked, the harbour held over 40 ships and six large seaplanes. (Historical Repository, HMAS Coonawarra, Darwin)

CHAPTER 2

– A DARWIN SKETCH

Australia had been at war since 1939. Her sailors, soldiers and airmen had distinguished themselves in many battles around the world, from fleet action in the Mediterranean, to air action over Britain, and in desert combat in the Middle East. But the war had not touched Australia's shores by January 1942. There had been no landings, no bombings, no action fought over Australia's soil. There had been action off Australia's shores, for units of the German Navy had carried out attacks by mine and surface raider – the November 1941 loss of the cruiser *HMAS Sydney* was a bitter blow to both the Royal Australian Navy and the country itself. While the attack on Pearl Harbor in December 1941 had launched the formidable Japanese armed forces into the war, as 1942 dawned there had been no attack against Australia by the Japanese. But in mid-January, with the deployment of four submarines to attack Darwin Harbour, the Imperial Japanese Navy was launching a potentially formidable attack against an unsuspecting Australia.

Darwin in early 1942 was a curious place. As the war against Germany had begun in 1939, the small town and its surrounding settlements had slowly shaken themselves into a semblance of a fighting base. However, the war was not taken too seriously – this might contradict the easy-going nature of life in the "Top End", a relaxed attitude probably essential for surviving the fierce heat and humidity. The harbour was defended by shore guns – the biggest 9.2-inch pair albeit unfinished – and a boom net which secured the huge harbour, three times the size of Sydney's, against submarines. But there were no fighter aircraft stationed at the Darwin airfields, and the Army's anti-aircraft guns were manned by new untested soldiers who were denied the ammunition even to practice.[1]

As far as naval operations went, Darwin itself had always been used more as a refueling base than as a centre for a permanent naval force, although the RAN had constructed several permanent buildings in the town, and in 1937 built to the south of Darwin a communications station: Naval Wireless Transmitting Station Coonawarra.[a] A Patrol Service with a small patrol

---

a   Naval WT Station Coonawarra was known as such or as the abbreviation NAVCOMSTA until the formal commissioning of *HMAS Coonawarra* on March 16, 1970.

craft – the *Larrakia* – was established, ironically captained by a RAAF Reservist, named CTG Haultain, who even more ironically took on a naval commission as the war intensified – he distinguished himself as a sterling commander of the corvette *HMAS Lithgow*.[2]

As the European war progressed the RAN's presence grew steadily larger, although it was at first confined to a sorry collection of requisitioned and/or ancient vessels. In 1940 a depot in the centre of Darwin was established and commissioned as *HMAS Melville*. Soon work began on the boom net, accompanied by the arrival of boom vessels *Kookaburra* and *Koala*, which were followed by a collection of coastal craft. The biggest ship in port unfortunately was the least mobile: *HMAS Platypus*, an old vessel of 3800 tons, which acted merely as a floating workshop. In December 1941 the RAN took over the two vessels of the Northern Territory Patrol Service, and the "Royal Darwin Navy" as the RAN's presence was humorously known, grew larger with the arrival of newly commissioned Navy corvettes. Bob Wallace, serving in *Warrnambool*, remembers, in addition to his own ship, working in Darwin with *Armidale*, *Kalgoorlie*, *Katoomba*, *Lithgow*, *Castlemaine* and *Townsville*. Once the war with Japan was declared, shipping movements in and out of the port were boosted enormously, often by American warships en route to operations. As a measure of this, it is significant that when the Japanese attacked on 19 February, 1942, over 40 ships were in the harbour.

Australian Navy operations in Darwin were largely the province of corvettes, the small "maids of all work" which were employed in huge numbers by the Royal Navy and to a total of 56 hulls by Australia's navy. Employed in mine-sweeping, shore gunfire support, anti-submarine warfare, anti-air warfare and according to some old sailors, anything else the local Naval Officer In Charge (NOIC) could think up, the corvettes' sturdy build and shallow draught made them well-suited to the shoal-filled and largely uncharted waters of northern Australia. Of particular note, once hostilities against the Japanese commenced in early December 1941, were escort duties for the army forces being taken north to take up a valiant but desperate fight against overwhelming Japanese numbers.[3]

More vessels continued to arrive after the commencement of the war against Japan. The boom net was only opened in daylight hours, recalled Able Seaman Harry Dale in his diary, written while serving on boom vessel *Karangi*. Somewhat different from the lot of a corvette's crew was the life of the boom sailors: they were based largely within the harbour on their small ships, but managed to make it ashore occasionally. Harry Dale's list of attractions included the canteen at the boom depot, which featured a tame rooster which drank beer, and the local tailor Lorna Lim's daughters, reputed by the sailors to be "very nice", although the girls were rarely seen.[b]

Upon arrival in Darwin any warship might be immediately employed on anti-submarine patrols,

---

b   Most civilians had been evacuated by 1942, at least officially. However, a number remained up to the February 1942 attack: Alan Powell in *The Shadow's Edge* gives a figure of over 2300 - see page 73.

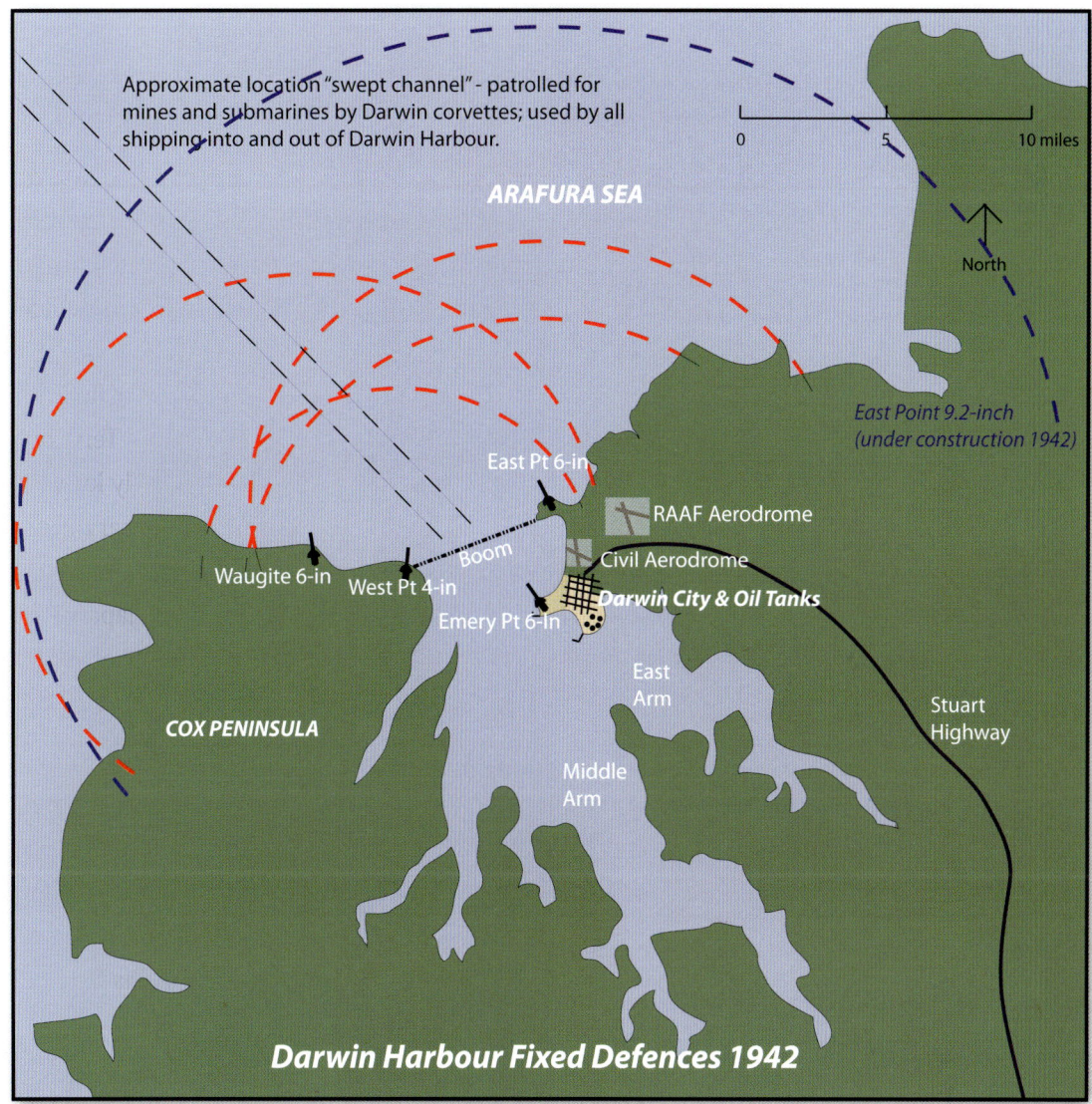

Approximate location "swept channel" - patrolled for mines and submarines by Darwin corvettes; used by all shipping into and out of Darwin Harbour.

0   5   10 miles

ARAFURA SEA

North

East Point 9.2-inch (under construction 1942)

East Pt 6-in

RAAF Aerodrome

Civil Aerodrome

Waugite 6-in   West Pt 4-in   Boom   **Darwin City & Oil Tanks**

Emery Pt 6-in

East Arm

COX PENINSULA

Stuart Highway

Middle Arm

Darwin Harbour Fixed Defences 1942

Darwin Harbour fixed defences early 1942: Shown are the effective ranges of the coastal artillery positions protecting Darwin Harbour, as well as the position of the Boom Net across the harbour entrance. Together these made for a relatively secure fleet base, with Darwin big enough to hold any number of vessels. Its large oil tanks, built pre-war, were intended for Commonwealth naval use, but it was the United States Asiatic Fleet that made Darwin its base during January 1942. Darwin was additionally important at this time as a supply route via Torres Strait to the Philippines or the Netherlands East Indies, so shipping movements through the small port were constant. The Boom Net was the longest in the world and required an entire fleet of small RAN vessels to keep it operational given the strong tides. Outside the ranges of the fixed defences of the port, the Japanese submarines lurked. (Peter Ingman)

Graphic by Peter Ingman

as the "duty escort" vessel or as the "immediate standby" ship, with occasional minesweeping duties. The ships' "Reports of Proceedings" give a picture of what must have been constant hard work, with the prospect of sudden action lurking uneasily in the back of everyone's minds. Relief from the duties was infrequent: sometimes occasioned by a special timetable such as "Sunday routine", where divisions, prayers and pay were followed by some leave. A holiday from seagoing might also be occasionally caused by maintenance requirements such as "cleaning boilers". Bill Hornery, serving in *HMAS Deloraine*, one of the ships prominent in this account, remembers how busy they were:

> ...*Deloraine* was hardly ever in the inner part of the harbour. We would come in - replenish with stores - and if not required for further duties we would proceed to West Arm and anchor there. Orders were either brought out by boat or if 'priority' sent by WT...

DARWIN IN STRATEGIC TERMS

Despite assurances that Australia would be defended by the Royal Navy in combination with the "Singapore Strategy", during the lean inter-war years Australian defence planners still had the foresight to build oil tanks at Darwin which would enable it to be used as an alternate fleet base.

When the RN's capital ships *Prince of Wales* and *Repulse* were sunk off Malaya just after the war began, this might have seemed an empty strategy. However, it was not without purpose. The US Asiatic Fleet commanders quickly realised that it would be annihilated if it remained near Manila, and so it withdrew to the south. By the start of January 1942, the Asiatic Fleet was based in Darwin, and briefly this location would be used for the purpose that pre-war planners intended.[4]

Despite most of Australia's fighting strength being deployed in the Middle East or elsewhere, in Australia itself slender resources had been employed in equipping the nation for the maritime war it had been fighting since 1939. The main threats were from surface raiders, submarines and mines. As a consequence after the Pacific war began the Darwin naval base had resources dedicated to combating each of these threats.[5]

Most significantly, a massive harbour boom was built across the entrance to the harbour. This was a floating fence, extending several miles and by far the longest in Australia. Maintenance of the boom was complicated by the strength and enormity of the huge tides in northern Australia – it was not uncommon for large gaps to be washed away for brief periods until repaired.

Indeed, for this reason, the RAN's entire strength of dedicated Boom Defence Vessels were directed to Darwin. By late January 1942, two vessels were serving as permanent gate vessels while three others were in service maintaining the boom itself. In addition, given the length of the boom, three newly commissioned ex-civilian motor cruisers were equipped with machine guns and small depth charges as a Boom Patrol. They would defend against special forces and midget submarine attacks.

For defence against mines, the 70th Auxiliary Minesweeper Squadron, consisting of a couple of converted civilian coasters (later three) maintained a swept channel into the harbour entrance. Darwin had no real anti-submarine capability until the arrival of *Bathurst*-class corvettes equipped with ASDIC sensors and depth charges.[6] A number of these had passed through Darwin on the way to Singapore during 1941.

The first vessel to serve operationally from Darwin was probably the corvette *HMAS Ballarat*, which escorted various convoys to and from Darwin in December 1941, and investigated a number of submarine contacts early in January 1942. On 5 January 1942 *HMAS Toowoomba* and *HMAS Wollongong* arrived in Darwin escorting some of the US "Pensacola Convoy" ships. However, these three corvettes quickly departed Darwin for Java on 11 January 1942. Then another corvette, *HMAS Deloraine*, arrived in Darwin. A week later, on 19 January 1942, *HMAS Lithgow* and *HMAS Katoomba* arrived in Darwin from Thursday Island, having escorted Convoy VK.1: US merchant ships *Meigs*, *Mauna Loa* and *Port Mar*. These three newly arrived corvettes formed the 24th Minesweeping Flotilla, and took part in the *I-124* action a few days later. The fact that these newly commissioned and newly arrived ships participated in such a major naval victory at this time was significant: much of this victory can be attributed to the high standards achieved by the young and expansionary RAN at this time.

During January 1942 the corvettes received much support from two RAN sloops, *HMAS Swan* and *HMAS Warrego*, which had arrived earlier in January. These were equipped for both anti-submarine and anti-aircraft defence, the early corvettes generally lacking the latter capability. As the corvettes accumulated at Darwin, the sloops were used more for seagoing escort duties than harbour defence.

Given the restricted wharf space at Darwin, great loads were placed upon the floating depot ship *HMAS Platypus*, and the newly created shore base *HMAS Melville*, which was not on the waterfront at Darwin but within the town itself. In addition a number of hastily requisitioned civilian craft helped maintain services within the harbour.

The small ships of the RAN helped set up and maintain several Army coastal defence positions both on the east and west side of Darwin Harbour – indeed those on the isolated west side were reliant on naval vessels for support. Such fortifications were relevant against surfaced submarines or other warships, and the deterrent effect during the war was successful: no enemy warship ever approached within range of these guns, nor did they appear to have ever been detected or targeted by enemy air forces.

The co-ordination between the air and naval forces was still a long way from being perfected. While the RAAF had capable maritime Lockheed Hudson "reconnaisance-bombers", these generally flew longer range missions and were needed far to the north of Darwin. The RAAF used short-ranged single-engined Wirraway aircraft for coastal patrols, but pre-war doctrine meant they could not fly more than 10 km from the coast. There is little record of them being involved in anti-submarine operations and they appear to have been weighted more towards beach patrols and Army cooperation duties.

This left a big gap in naval aviation at Darwin. All of the RAAF flying boats were employed on the east coast and around New Guinea and surrounding islands. The RAAF lacked such aircraft in Darwin and for that reason a solitary floatplane of the USN Patrol Wing 10, operating from *USS Langley* in Darwin harbour, has a significant impact in this story. Unlike the Wirraways, it was trained to operate and communicate directly with naval vessels.[c]

Above all it can be argued that the naval response to the submarine and mine threats at Darwin was adequate. Despite much increased surface traffic, the RAN re-directed maritime trade routes away from focal mining points and quickly organised convoys. This was done quickly with the co-operation of the USN and was successful as not a single vessel was lost ... although the margin of comfort was very thin.

US Asiatic Fleet

Despite the grand title, the US Asiatic Fleet had no capital ships. Aside from such vessels as the Chinese river gunboats that were hastily withdrawn to Manila and where possible southwards again, this force consisted mainly of WWI-era destroyers, a respectable number of mainly newly arrived submarines, and support vessels. The flagship was the capable 8-inch gun cruiser *USS Houston*, over 600 feet long and with her clipper bow described as "one of the most beautiful ships in the navy".[7] *Houston* would subsequently become closely linked with both Darwin and an RAN cruiser, *HMAS Perth*. The older light cruiser *USS Marblehead* and the more modern light cruiser *USS Boise* were also attached to the Asiatic Fleet at the outbreak of the war.

After southern withdrawal, all of these vessels would spend time in Darwin during January 1942. The first USN convoy, escorted by *Houston* and various destroyers, arrived in Darwin in late December 1941. With their own oilers and support ships, they barely needed the overwhelmed wharfage facilities. *USS Marblehead*, the ex-carrier *USS Langley* and other vessels arrived on 3 January 1942, followed a few days later by *Boise* and various support vessels. During the month there was a constant shuttling of USN convoys between Darwin and various locations within the NEI and Torres Strait to the east. This meant that during January 1942 there were usually a number of WWI-era "flush-decker" or "four-piper" destroyers in Darwin such as *USS Edsall* and *USS Peary* – both would become especially associated with the port.

This then was a busy port, full of warships and fighting men, but in a location that had not yet seen enemy action. There had been plenty of rumours, possibilities and false alarms: a RAN chronology of naval events in the north reports on 1 January 1942 a: "registration on underwater indicator loops indicated a Japanese submarine entered Darwin Harbour on a reconnaissance of shipping in the port". However, the calm before the storm was soon to break. To the north, the Imperial Japanese Navy's four vessels of the 6th Submarine Squadron were on their way south to contain and sink the many ships that then called Darwin home.[c]

(Endnotes)

1   See Mulholland, Jack. *Darwin Bombed*. Mulholland describes in first person terms the limitations of the defence. Robert Rayner's comprehensive *The Army and the Defence of Darwin Fortress* gives exact details.

2   Haultain, CTG. *Watch off Arnhem Land. The* Northern Territory Patrol Service eventually acquired the *Kuru* as well.

3   For example, see Gull Force, 2/21st.Battalion Association's History at http://www.gullforce.org.au/Battalion_History.html 8 September 2010.

4   Gill, G. Hermon. *Royal Australian Navy 1939-1942*, Australia in the War of 1939-1945, Series Two Navy, Volume I. Canberra: Australian War Memorial, 1957. (p.589)

5   *HMAS Melville* War Diary; Australian War Memorial; Series Number AWM 78; Control symbol 400/2.

6   Stevens, David, Papers in Australian Maritime Affairs No.15, *A Critical Vulnerability – The Impact of the submarine on Australia's Maritime Defence 1915-1954*. Commonwealth of Australia.

7   Winslow, WG. *The Fleet the Gods Forgot – The Asiatic Fleet in WWII*. Maryland, USA: Naval Institute Press, 1982. (p.13)

c   The term "squadron'" seems also to appear as "division" in various writings of the period. Translators sometimes seem to translate the Japanese word as "corps"; occasionally as "squadron" or "division". This book follows the practice of the more authorative books and uses "squadron" throughout to describe the group of four minelayers.

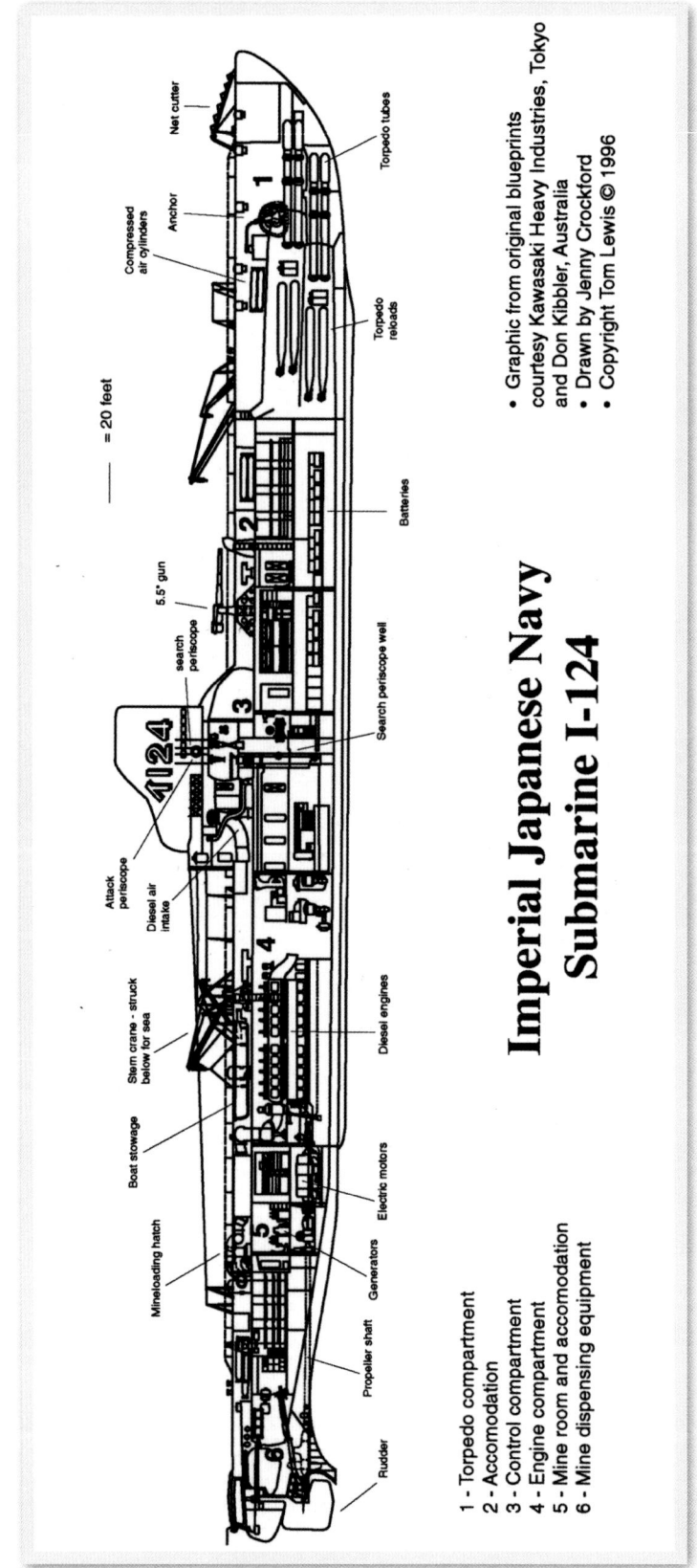

Imperial Japanese Navy Submarine I-124

• Graphic from original blueprints courtesy Kawasaki Heavy Industries, Tokyo and Don Kibbler, Australia
• Drawn by Jenny Crockford
• Copyright Tom Lewis © 1996

1 - Torpedo compartment
2 - Accomodation
3 - Control compartment
4 - Engine compartment
5 - Mine room and accomodation
6 - Mine dispensing equipment

CHAPTER 3

– NAVAL COMBATANTS – SUBMARINE VERSUS CORVETTE

A diesel-electric submarine, the originally-named *I-24* was one of four older model boats that formed the sixth Japanese submarine squadron. The first of the boats was built by the Kawasaki Company, south of Tokyo, but after financial difficulties, the second and third boats were finished in the Kure Navy yards. The *I-24* remained at Kobe, but was finished by workers from the Naval Construction Department, and completed in December 1928, some two years after being laid down.

The four boats of the squadron were modeled on a German U-boat, the *U-125*. This was a design described as "UEII Project 45", with *U-117* as the first boat of the class. *U-125* was one of seven from the surrendered German fleet provided to Japan after World War 1 as part of reparations. During the World War 1 these German boats had not proved capable. They were based on a UEI class called Project 43, and the new design was modified[I] to carry 42 mines internally and extra torpedoes and mines externally; the latter to be moved on rails to their launching position aft. But the design of the two horizontal 100cm minelaying tubes, a bigger mine room and associated equipment, placed between the propellers and the conning tower, had meant, as Eberhard Rossler tells us in *U-Boat: the Evolution and Technical History of German Submarines* "the profile and cross-section measurements of the pressure hull had to be changed several times". This contributed to the German boats' poor sea-keeping qualities, all of which were to be passed along to the Japanese copy. The *U-125* served as the Japanese submarine *O1*, and after being used as the basis for copying, was broken up at Kure in 1922.

I-124 was longer than its German predecessors, at 279 feet being 85.04 metres, whereas Rossler cites the Project 45 boats as being 81.5 metres in length. The extra "moment arm" would have contributed even more difficulty to efforts to keep the bow and stern of the boat straight and level; a design flaw to which this class of minelaying submarines was particularly prone.

Japanese submarines were not given a name, unlike many British and American submarines of WWII, but rather a number. The submarines were in three groups, and the first group – the large, or first-class submarines – were given the prefix イ, which is the second character in one of the

Mochitsura Hashimoto (right) standing on the casing of a submarine during the 1950s with Lieutenant Commander Teruaki Kawano. Kawano eventually became a distinguished scholar, specialising in maritime history, at the National Institute for Defence Studies, Tokyo. (Teruiki Kawano)

Japanese alphabets. The coastal short range submarines were given a "Ro" prefix, the second character in the same alphabet, and the midget "Kaiten" submarines were given the third letter: "Ha". Therefore the "I-class" designation by which many Allied nations described the bigger Japanese submarines was not entirely accurate, but was to become widely accepted.

In 1938 two new classes of submarine – the *I-15* and *I-16* series – were also being built. To avoid confusion with these vessels, a 100 prefix number was given to the four minelaying boats. Accordingly, the boat launched as *I-24* became *I-124*.

The basic performance, configuration and weapon-fit of *I-124* differ in many publications. A compilation version of *Jane's Fighting Ships* for World War II gives one snapshot:

> *I* 124 (ex *I*-24) (Dec 12, 1927). All by Kawasaki Co., Kobe....
> - Displacement: 1,142/1,470 tons. Dimensions: 279.5 x 24.75 x 14.25 feet.
> - Armament: 1-5.5 inch, 4-21" tubes, 42 mines.
> - Machinery: Diesels, H.P. 2,400 = 14 kts. Electric motors H.P. 1,200 = 9 .5 kts.
> - Design believed to be based on German UB types.

One of the most famous Japanese submarine commanders of World War II gives a set of slightly different figures. Mochitsura Hashimoto had a distinguished war record, which included sinking the American cruiser *Indianapolis*, the flagship of Admiral Spruance, Commander of the Fifth Fleet, although he was not on board[a] at the time – the ship being under the command of Captain CB McVay III. Hashimoto produced his own account of the submarine fleet's campaign in *Sunk. The Story of the Japanese Submarine Fleet* in 1954. He describes the *I-121* class somewhat differently:

- Displacement: 1,142 tons.
- Guns: One 15 cm.
- Torpedoes: 12 (estimated). Equipped for laying 42 mines.
- Surface speed: 14.5 knots.
- Range: 10, 500 nautical miles @ 8 knots.
- Safety depth (feet): 195.
- Crew: 44

It might be noted here that there has always been some confusion over *I-124*'s crewing: the figure given above is more comparable with the German amount of men carried, while reports on *I-124* vary by almost double that amount. The Japanese Embassy in Canberra advised in 1995 that their version of the figure was 80 men. This would constitute the crew of that vessel, and the staff of Squadron Commander Endo.

A final picture of *I-124*'s vital statistics might be best therefore gained from a combination of original sources. The following relies on information as given in the Japanese post-war publication *Nihon Kaigun Sensuikan Shi (A History of the Imperial Japanese Navy Submarine)*, and amended by Commodore (Ret.) Kennosuke Torisu, Imperial Japanese Navy 1927-45, Chief of Staff of the IJN's Sixth Fleet.

This consensus gives the submarine's displacement as 1, 383 tons surfaced and 1, 768 submerged. Her overall length was 279 feet, with a breadth of 24.5 ft. Performance figures give a speed of 14.5 knots on the surface; seven knots submerged; and a maximum dive depth of 195 feet. The boat's two diesels produced a total of 2,400 horsepower, with twin electric motors giving 1, 200 horsepower; the twin propellers able to drive her 10, 500 miles at eight knots. (The electric motors in a diesel-electric submarine drive the boat underwater, as the diesels need large quantities of air to run; air in short supply and needed for the crew. The electric motors run off batteries, which have been charged by the diesels. However, the motors drain the batteries, which means that sooner or later the submarine will lose its propulsion power.)

Additional information of interest related to *I-124* is that she carried some of her war stores between the outer hull and the inner pressure hull. Much of the boat's mine and torpedo load was

---

a   The commander of a task force or fleet does not "captain" one of the ships. As the reader will see in the deployment of the *I-124* submarine and her sisters, the commander "flies his flag" in one of the ships, which is required to house both him and his staff, often leading to accommodation problems.

A somewhat foreshortened view of I-124 running on the surface. Features of interest include the large hatch at the stern – probably part of the mine-loading equipment – and the net cutter at the bow. (Maritime History Department, Japanese Self-Defence Agency)

stored in this way, to be installed in the stern minelaying tubes or forward torpedo tubes when inner stocks were exhausted; according to authorities such as Commodore Torisu, eight torpedo reloads were carried there. The torpedoes were probably the Type 89, 900lb. model, capable of 10, 000 yards at a speed of 49 knots, or alternatively, 13, 000 yards at 45 knots.

The four boats of the minelaying squadron underwent some modification after they were completed. As they were long-range vessels it was considered by the Navy that they would be used in very distant locations, and a dual role was anticipated: not only would these boats be used in an anti-shipping role, they could also be used to refuel seaplanes. Consequently, in 1940 the four boats of the Sixth Squadron were modified to carry refueling tanks on their upper deck.

Japan had been steadily building a submarine fleet before she committed herself to war. The number of submarines she possessed was large for a medium power, perhaps in reaction to the capital ship limitations that had been a result of the Five Power Naval Armaments Treaty of 1922. At the beginning of Japan's hostilities against the Allies she had around 60 submarines – some accounts say 63 or 64. Fourteen of these boats were 500-1000ton vessels designed mainly for offshore work, and designated as the RO class. The イ -class vessels were made up of 20 large fleet boats; plus 22 submarines designed for special work such as carrying midget submarines or aircraft, and the four boats designed for minelaying. During the war Japan was to build another 126 submarines – a substantial fleet curiously not used to anywhere near its potential.

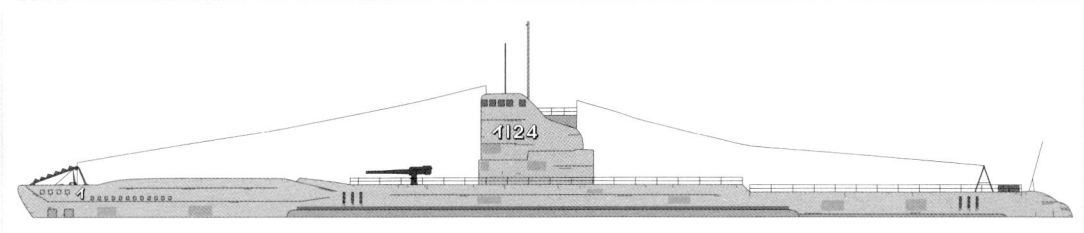

I-124
MINELAYING PATROL SUBMARINE

Laid down: 1926; launched Dec 1927; completed Dec 1928

Dimensions: Length: 279 feet; Width: 24 feet 5 inches; Draught: 14 feet 6 inches

Displacement: 1,142 tons standard; 1,383 tons surfaced; 1,768 submerged

Construction: steel; inner pressure hull; outer free flooding hull

Armament: 1 x 5.5-inch deck gun; 4 x 21-inch bow torpedo tubes; 12 x Type 89 torpedo reloads;
    42 x Type 88 mines (960 kg each)
    I-124 could also be configured with external fuel tanks for refuelling seaplanes

Performance: 14.5 knots surfaced; 7.5 knots submerged; safety diving depth 195 feet

Range: 10, 500 nm at 8 knots (surfaced); 40 nm at 4.5 knots (submerged)

Engines: 2-shaft diesels 2, 400 hp total; two electric motors 1, 200 hp total

Complement: 80 officers and men

I-124 was the fourth and last of a class of minelaying submarines built in Japan during the 1920s. A copy of a WWI German design, they inherited several design defects making them poor sea boats and difficult to control underwater. Nevertheless their long range and well-trained crews made them a potentially potent force at the start of WWII. By 1943 they were recognised as unsuitable for frontline service and the two surviving members of the class were withdrawn to Japan and used for training.   Graphic by Peter Ingman

Alongside the more modern boats – a submarine is always a "boat"[b] – the mine-laying vessels were a dated design. As the four were a direct copy of a German U-boat of World War I vintage, they shared many of the ideas of submarine design from that earlier struggle.

If submarine design is studied against a timeline, some obvious trends can be seen, and the minelaying boats' design places them in the early years of the 20th century rather than the 1930s. Hull design and characteristics are two criteria for judging submarine design success. Modern boats are streamlined for two reasons: speed and silence. Submarines today are usually faster when completely submerged than when cruising with their conning tower / fin / sail[c] exposed. The modern hull follows a teardrop design, with rounded bow merging smoothly into tapered

b   The reason a submarine is called a boat is historical. Early submarines were the size of small boats rather than ships, and hence called as such. The term "pig boat" was also in use as slang, perhaps referring to both the smell of a shut-down submarine and the procedure of surfacing and submerging constantly, rather like the "sea pig" – a dolphin. By the time submarines became bigger the term had stuck, and submariners, who were developing the traditions of a new marque of warship, were fiercely protective of this "tradition", just as they still are – a Jolly Roger is flown by submarines who are returning to port after a kill, for example. *HMS Conqueror* flew this flag after her victory over the cruiser *General Belgrano* in the Falklands war.

c   The terms of conning tower, fin and sail are often confused. They all refer to the same idea - the tower centrally placed above a submarine's hull that carries a myriad of aerials, periscopes, "snort" tubes, even TV cameras. The modern term is usually either of the last two. This book uses the term conning tower when describing World War II boats. The conning tower on these boats was not part of the pressure hull.

stern. Every aspect of the hull is designed so that neither is speed hindered, nor is noise created by unnecessary disturbance of the water, for a submarine's life may depend on her ability to slip silently away from her enemies.

Nearly a century of changes in design can be seen by visitors to submarines today. Hulls are smooth and streamlined. Often there are very few openings or even indentations in the hull, which itself may be covered in sound-absorbent tiles. Modern conventional diesel/electric submarines are much "quieter" than their WWII counterparts, and even the nuclear boats – which by design can often be noisier than the diesel/electrics because of the need to constantly run reactor cooling pumps – have been able to take advantage of absorbent tiles and other innovations to become remarkably sonar-quiet. Submarine underwater speeds are often in excess of those achieved by surface warships: some modern nuclear attack submarines are capable of speeds well in excess of 30 knots. Designed to spend almost all of their patrol time underwater, the whole concept of a submarine is now different from that envisaged by designers in the first half of the century, who saw submarines as spending the majority of their time on the surface, submerging only to avoid detection by enemies within the immediate vicinity.

So by comparison with ideas reflected by today's philosophies, *I-124*'s design was very different. Like almost all submarines of the two world wars, she carried a gun forward of her conning tower. She was big; about the same length as a modern navy frigate. Her hull was covered with plates, holes, indentations, cavities and hatches, all of which slowed her down and made her more vulnerable to underwater listening devices.

To make matters worse, the minelaying submarines were poor performers in the essential business of staying submerged. Hashimoto is not complimentary:

> Submarines I.121, 122, 123, and 124 were specially equipped for mine-laying duties. In addition to the bow tubes, the stem of the boat was specially adapted for laying mines....In 1940 they were equipped with petrol tanks on the upper deck for refueling aircraft, and were thus able to carry out an additional role. Their peculiar construction made them very difficult boats to handle. Their surface speed was slow and they were difficult to manoeuvre submerged, owing to their small hydroplanes and rudders. The slightest difference in weight forward or aft gave them a list.[d] If the least bit lightened they tended to surface and if made over-heavy they tended to sink. They were known throughout the service as the "Dreaded submarines".

---

d The terms "stem" of the boat, and "The slightest difference in weight forward or aft gave them a list" are perhaps mistakes in translation. "Stem" is probably "stern" and "list" should be "pitch" as when a submarine or ship "lists" this refers to a sideways movement rather than a tilt or pitch bow-down or up.

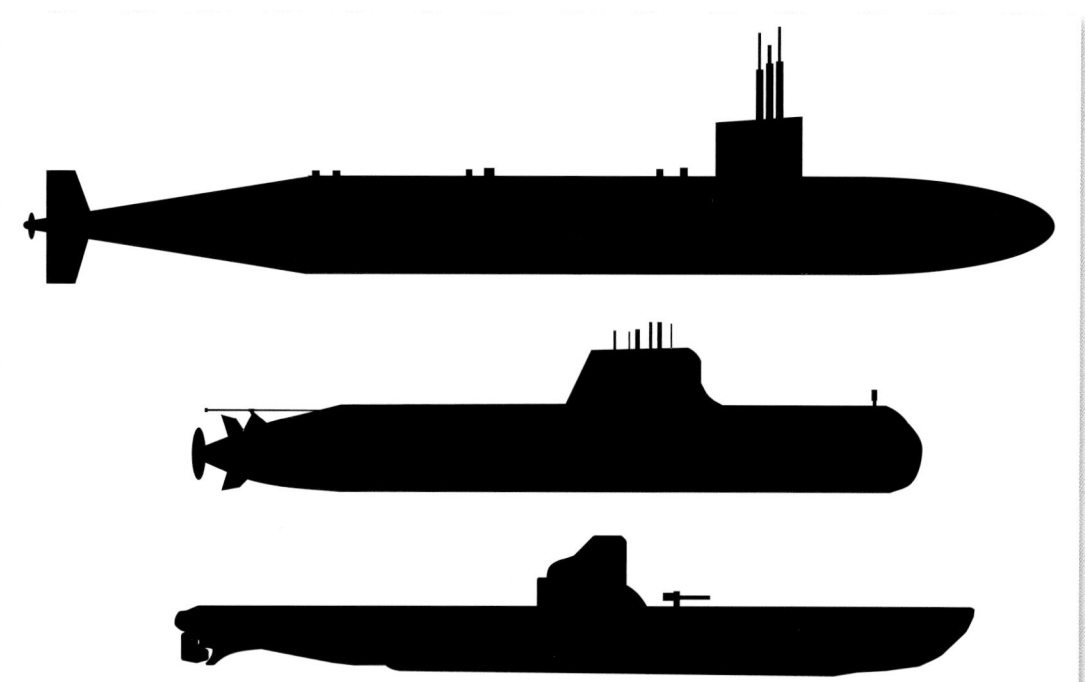

The old and the new. Pictured top is a Los Angeles-class nuclear attack submarine profile; centre a conventional RAN Collins-class submarine, while lower is I-124, reflecting WWI and II technology. Drawn to scale, it is perhaps surprising that the overall dimensions of large ocean-going submarines have not changed greatly in this time. However, the Los Angeles-class (6,900 tons) and the Collins-class (3,050 tons) have much larger displacements than I-124 (1,142 tons), packing a lot more into their efficient, streamlined cylindrical hulls. The converse of modern submarine thinking, I-124 was designed primarily for surface cruising with relatively short periods underwater. The I-124 profile can be misleading: underneath the profile of her upper deck was an unpressurised storage area cluttered with boats, derricks, mines and other equipment. Her actual hull was slimmer than the profile shows, reflecting her much lighter displacement.

Graphic by Peter Ingman

I served as torpedo officer of one of these craft in 1940. When a mine was dropped, a compensatory weight of water had to be let in, otherwise the stern would break surface. If too much water were let in, the boat would sink. The forty-eight[e] mines had to be moved one by one to the tail of the boat, while water was pumped to the fore-end to prevent the boat from becoming tail heavy – a really dangerous task. Some accidents due to faulty procedure were reported, including casualties caused by the sudden movement of mines due to bad trimming...It was extremely difficult to keep the boat level and at the prescribed depth, and at the same time lay the mines in the correct positions. Usually the mines had to be laid with a two-knot tide running at the entrance to bays, and very careful co-operation between captain and navigator was necessary to avoid any dangerous error. [(p. 39/40)]

---

e   Hashimoto in an earlier reference discusses submarine *I-6* which laid mines off Brisbane. He describes how "two or three were carried in each tube". If this practice was carried out in the minelaying boats, this would give *I-124* a capacity to carry 42 mines plus three in each tube, thus explaining his reference to 48 mines here.

The mines themselves were extremely heavy, awkward devices. The Type 88 mine weighed 960 kilograms each. The release of just one meant almost a tonne of seawater had to be pumped in to compensate for each release. The explosive charge was only 180kg, with the rest of the weapon made up of the casing and mooring chains and an anchor. [2]

The operational release of a mine could have serious consequences. Firing a torpedo or laying a mine would mean some of the submarine's negative buoyancy would be lost whenever that action was taken – perhaps rising unexpectedly to the surface in close proximity to enemy warships. As if matters were not bad enough, contemporary accounts of life in the submarine fleet do not make it sound pleasant. Conditions were even more cramped than they were on German or Allied submarines, and fresh food was normally gone after a week at sea. Life on board one of the minelayer submarines, given all of these attendant problems, was more to be endured than enjoyed.

THE OPPONENT – THE *BATHURST* CLASS CORVETTE

Like her sister ships in the *Bathurst* class, *Deloraine* was a tough little ship, armed with a variety of weapons that changed throughout the course of the war. Sixty of these vessels were built in Australian shipyards during the war – 56 for the RAN and four for the Indian Navy – and they carried out a variety of duties, ranging from convoy escort to troop transport and the occasional mine-sweep, for they were similar to the British "Bangor" class which had started off designed as a minesweeper. Named after Australian towns, the first was named after Bathurst, so the corvettes became the *Bathurst*-class. Many of the ships were produced in Sydney or Melbourne, but as the war went on they were produced in many areas, with 1944 seeing one corvette being launched every 26 days.

Dan Studeman, who served for three years in the class, described them in his book *A Small War*, as:

> ...the work-horses of the Fleet, a task they were eminently suited for, being very handy ships, shallow draft, and, for those days, a reasonable turn of speed, exceptionally good sea boats and well crewed. (p. 1)

The corvettes were built from steel, had a displacement of 650 tons, and were 186 feet in length. Their beam was 31 feet, and they had a draught of eight feet, six inches, making them particularly suitable for work close to shores.

Armament was either one 4" gun or a 12 pounder gun, one 40mm gun, and five or six machine guns. Frank Marsh remembers *Deloraine* as starting off life with: "...a 12 pounder "ack ack"

HMAS Deloraine in Sydney Harbour. (Royal Australian Navy)

gun forward...", and fellow corvette crewmen such as Bill Price and Bob Wallace confirm the original fitting of a 12 pounder. Frank Marsh goes on to specify the rest of the armament: "On each wing of bridge, one Lewis MG & one Vickers .5 MG (water cooled)". The machine guns were later replaced, according to Marsh, with Oerlikons, with a Bofors 40mm replacing one of these aft at a later date. The bridge itself was closed, although some ships of the class had an open bridge, the converse of their British sister, with their closed bridge probably a blessing in the cold waters of the North Sea and the North Atlantic, and a welcome relief to anyone who had served on the Flower class corvettes, which featured an open bridge, a very cold solution to the problem of visibility obscured by ice.

For its anti-submarine role, the corvette was fitted with two depth charge throwers aft plus two "roll outs": rails that allowed the depth charges to be rolled over the stern. The throwers threw the depth charges to port and starboard. About 40 – some sailors suggest up to 60 – depth charges, each weighing quarter of a ton, were carried. Bob Wallace makes the point that the last six corvettes built, "the wholly anti-submarine versions", had four throwers.

Range could be a comprehensive 6, 000 miles at a slow speed of four to five knots, dropping to about 4, 000 miles at higher speeds. The corvette's top speed was 15-16 knots – insufficient to allow them to chase many types of enemy warships, but enough to escort convoys or chase submerged submarines. While the official crew complement was 60, in wartime the corvettes often carried up to 100 men when engaged on the diverse duties the RAN required, and also in response to the ever-expanding range of specialised equipment; for example radar, which was fitted in successive refits. In these early days they filled a vital gap in Australia's defences, and despite their inadequacies performed very well. Bob Wallace again:

> As anti-submarine platforms they were inadequate, as anti-aircraft vessels they were very poorly armed initially but greatly improved later - as minesweepers they were ideal...they were all we had available and acquitted themselves admirably under the circumstances.

Deloraine was a brand new ship, having only just been commissioned on 23 November 1941. Having completed her sea trials by Christmas Day she was due to sail for Darwin, but according to the ship's Leading Telegraphist Bill Hornery she was delayed by "gremlins in the compass" and departed on Boxing Day. *Deloraine* was carrying a crew of 75, under the command of Lieutenant Commander Menlove, RANR(S), and his five officers, who were all members of the Naval Reserve, and therefore possessing a variety of backgrounds. They were not to know that awaiting her was to be a deadly duel with a submarine; the beginning of a career that would see her go on to become one of the more famous RAN ships of the war.

Hornery has described *Deloraine*'s first voyage in an article written for *HMAS Scuttlebutt*, the journal of the Ballina section of the Naval Association of Australia. The corvette proceeded north from Sydney to Brisbane and then Townsville, where the crew enjoyed a brief two-day stopover. After steaming around the northern coastline *Deloraine* arrived in Darwin on 7 January, 1942. Her duties, as for all of the local corvettes, were to be many and varied: minesweeping, anti-submarine patrols and escort duties.

While her crew were a mix of experienced sailors and new hands, they had been exercised on the voyage north: the Commanding Officer's report of the voyage lists drills in "night action stations", exercises with the "12 pounder gun" and in general a satisfactory voyage, although he expressed concern that the ship's fuel-consumption was higher than the builder's specifications. In short, the ship and her crew were as ready for war as their short preparation time would allow.

(Endnotes)

1   See authorities such as Anthony Preston and John Batchelor in *The First Submarines,*

2   Campbell, John. *Naval Weapons of World War Two*. Naval Institute Press, Annapolis, USA, 2007. (p.213)

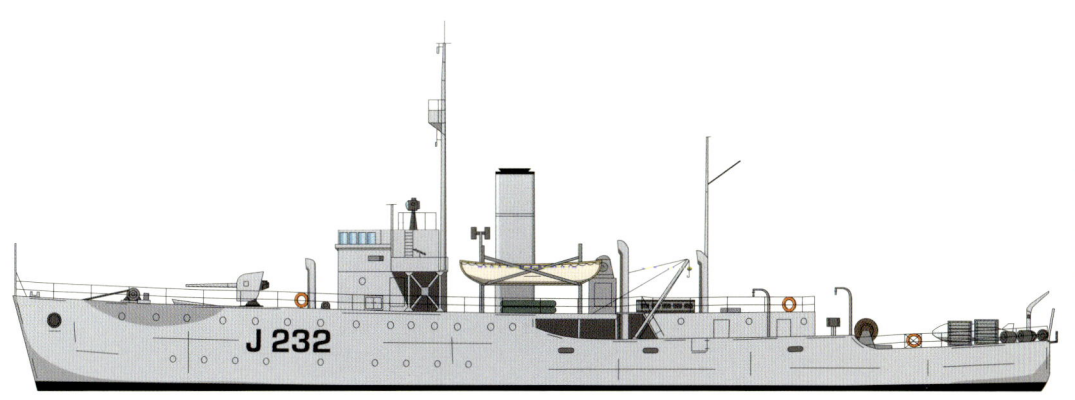

HMAS DELORAINE

Type: Bathurst-class corvette (formal designation AMS "Australian Minesweeper")

Builder: Mort's Dock and Engineering Co Ltd, Sydney

Commissioned: 22 November 1941

Displacement: 650 tons　　　　**Length:** 186 feet　　　　**Beam:** 31 feet　　Draught 8 feet 6 inches

Armament (early 1942): 1 x 12-pounder gun (3-inch)

        Lewis & Vickers machine guns (on bridge wings)

        2 x Thornycroft Depth Charge throwers (port & starboard)

        Stern Depth-Charge rails

        20 - 35 Depth Charges (420 lb total weight each)

Sensors / Equipment: ASDIC sonar dome fitted underneath hull

        Minesweeping gear including French Floats carried aft

Main Machinery: Triple expansion, 2 shafts

Horsepower: 2,000 IHP　　　　**Speed:** 15 knots　　　　**Complement:** 85

The Bathurst-class "corvette" was a wholly Australian design, able to be built quickly in several local shipyards. Sixty were built, 56 serving with the RAN. Named after Australian towns, while formally designated as minesweepers, they were also capable anti-submarine vessels although lacking the performance of destroyers.

Graphic by Peter Ingman

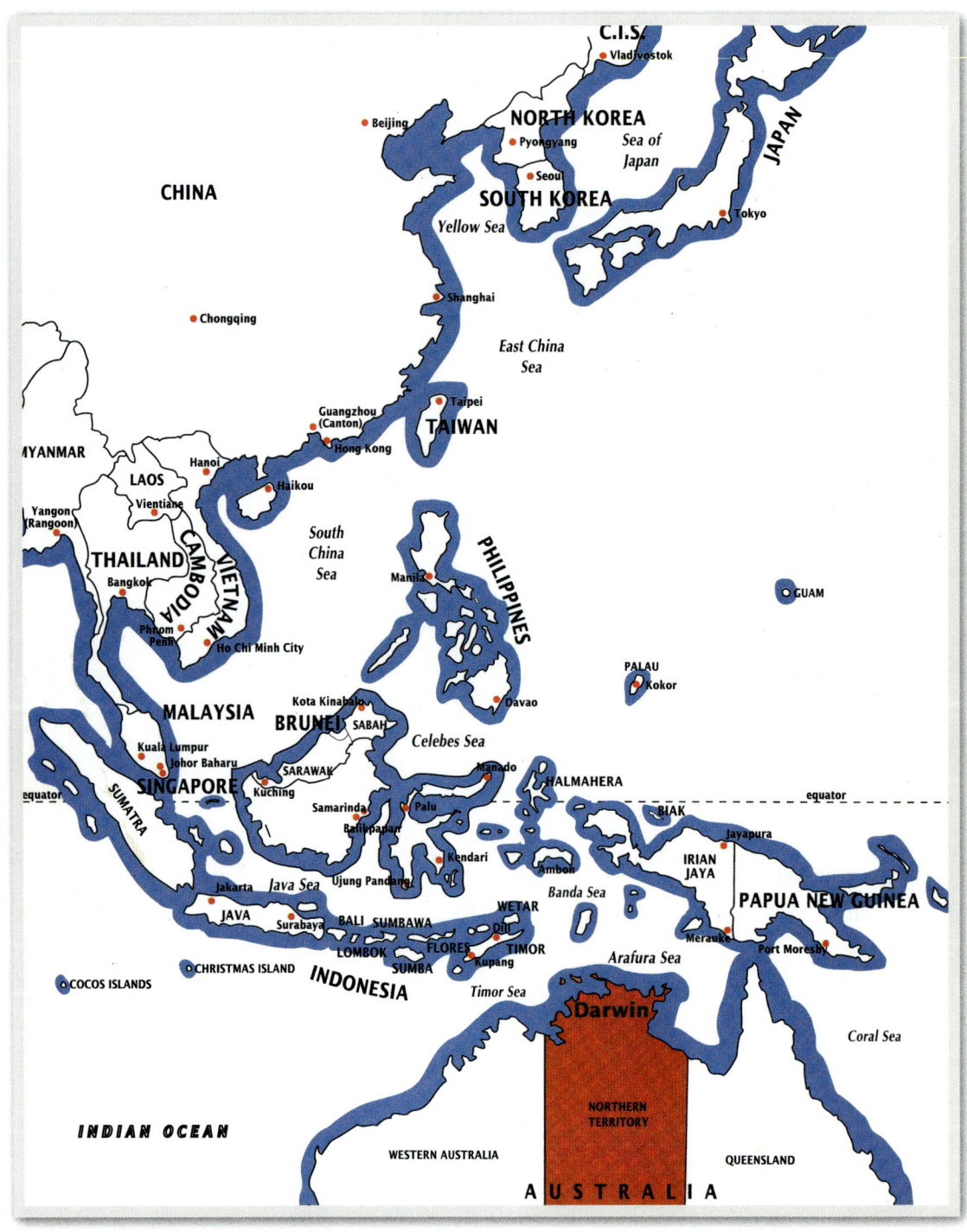

Darwin and the South-East Asian region (NT Department of Asian Relations and Industry and the Trade Development Zone Authority)

CHAPTER 4

– A STRATEGIC PICTURE

Japan possessed a submarine fleet of considerable size before World War II. On the commencement of hostilities in December 1941 the Imperial Navy had 64 submarines. During the war another 126 were built, making the IJN by any Western standard a very powerful adversary. However, Japan did not use her submarine weapon to its full advantage during the war. Military historian Masanori Ito, writing in his 1956 publication *The End of the Imperial Japanese Navy,* commented:

> In spite of its size, spirit and reputation, this redoubtable force proved to be an almost total failure. At war's end not more than 50 Japanese submarines were still in existence, and most of them were inoperable because of damage or lack of maintenance. The rest had vanished, achieving little more than a remarkable score for the enemy. (p. 24)

There were a number of reasons for this lack of success. Rather than using the fleet for pursuing one aim, as the U-boats were used in wolf pack tactics that nearly won for Germany the Battle of the Atlantic, for example, the Japanese submarine fleet was employed on a variety of interesting but ultimately largely ineffective tasks, ranging from deploying seaplanes, midget submarines and *kaitens* – the human torpedoes – to acting as seaplane refuelers and underwater transports. The submarine captains themselves could have strangled nations by attacking the vital freighters, troop transports or oil tankers that sustained the war effort in the Pacific. Instead they largely attacked the Allied warships – whether through their training as warriors instinctively or deliberately seeking out ship to ship combat, or whether having this decision made for them on a high command level is an interesting debate.

Some blame for this disappointing result is identified by Masanori Ito as the boats themselves:

> One of the main causes for this submarine failure was the lack of habitability in the boats. Too much emphasis was placed on making it a war machine, and not enough on living conditions for the crew who had a minimum of space and creature comfort. The confined quarters might have been adequate if there had

I-122 makes rendezvous with a flying boat in peacetime. Note the awning rigged forward of the conning tower.
(Maritime History Department, Japanese Self-Defence Agency)

been enough men to rotate the crews for proper rest and rehabilitation after each mission. But there were never enough trained men....Training in homeland waters had not prepared them for Arctic and tropic extremes, where men and machine betrayed unexpected weaknesses. The results were disastrous. [p. 24]

The submarine fleet could have made a significant alteration to the results of the war if they had been deployed effectively. From February 1942, the fleet was armed for the war with a fast, oxygen-propelled torpedo that left no tell-tale stream of bubbles in its wake. Its captains possessed daring, courage and ability in all the right measures: the penetration of Sydney Harbour by midget submarines and the bombing of the American coast by submarine-deployed seaplane were two of the more visible testimonies to those qualities. The general consensus of naval historians' opinion shows that if the submarine fleet had been used more appropriately, significant battles of the war might have had a different result, perhaps even that the overall result of the war or the date of the final outcome might have been different.

Polmar and Carpenter, authors of *Submarines of the Imperial Japanese Navy*, for example, suggest that submarines could have been far more effectively deployed at both Pearl Harbor and Midway. Further, as naval historian David Stevens points out in "The last Japanese submarine off Australia", the German U-boats sunk 2, 840 merchant ships during the war; the

IJN submarines only 184. He further comments:

> ...on a strategic level Japanese submarine doctrine was fundamentally flawed. Too often submarines were employed on inappropriate missions or in a piecemeal fashion. They were never given the resources, priority and freedom they needed to achieve significant results. (p. 40)

But misused or not, the IJN's submariners went to war brave and determined. Submarine *I-124*'s final mission portrayed just these aspects: in shallow water, commanding an outdated and unstable submarine her captain was to attack a modern warship and only just miss being successful. Earlier that morning her sister ship *I-123* was to attack an escorted convoy in the same area, in a shallow section of the ocean with sonar conditions favouring his opponent. The captains could have avoided action in these confined waters but instead of waiting for a lucky chance bravely chose the greater certainty of combat – and with it, accepted the possibility of death and defeat.

The minelaying boats, forming the 6th Submarine Squadron, under the supervision of Commander Keiyu Endo, were commanded as follows:

> *I-121*: Commander Shinobu Endo;
>
> *I-122*: Lieutenant Commander Hidejiro Utsuki;
>
> *I-123*: Lieutenant Commander Toshitake Ueno;
>
> *I-124*: Lieutenant Commander Kouichi Kishigami.

I-124's war career was to be brief but violent. She began the conflict by sailing from Hainan Island, off Southern China, on 1 December, 1941. According to the Japanese publication *Nihon Kaigun Sensuikan Shi*, and with some later confirmation by Japanese Embassy officials in Canberra, *I-124* laid 39 mines near Manila Bay on the evening of 7 December.

I-124 then settled down and waited. On 10 December, at 0100, a British ship, the 1523 ton *SS Hareldawins,* was sunk by one of the mines. This is claimed by some as the first vessel sunk by any Japanese submarine in the war. The Japanese report refers to two more sinkings claimed from *I-124*'s mines, both on 17 December: the United States vessel *Corregidor* (1, 881 tons) – "blown to splinters with heavy loss of life" – and the *Panamanian Daylight*, of 1, 976 tons.

Hashimoto's book does not agree with the first-sinking claim: suggesting instead that this distinction goes to *I-26*, which "sank a 3, 000 ton military transport by gunfire, scoring the first kill by a Japanese submarine in the war."(34). Hashimoto also suggests that *I-124* "rescued aircraft crews who had crashed in the air attack on Manila, and was also engaged in sending out weather reports."(p. 40)

I-124 withdrew from the area and on 14 December arrived at Cam Ranh Bay, reuniting with the other three boats of the minelaying squadron under the command of Rear Admiral Chimaki Kono. On the 18th *I-124* left the Bay for patrol in the South China Sea and on the 26th December the submarine met up with *I-123*. On New Year's Eve they both arrived in Davao, in the Philippines, to meet the Squadron flagship, the submarine depot ship *Chogei*.

The new year of 1942 arrived and the Japanese war machine was relentlessly sweeping south. The port of Darwin – a base from which the Allies could consolidate and strike back – was recognised as being a target that might be usefully attacked. The *I-121* and *I-122* both left Davao on the 5th. On January 11 at 0400, the *I-121* carried out an unsuccessful torpedo attack on a destroyer – the Allied ship's identity is unknown. The following morning *I-121* laid 37 mines west of Bathurst Island. Meanwhile *I-122* had journeyed to the Torres Strait area and three days later was laying 30 mines in the Torres Strait. Both submarines then headed north again and on the 18th to the north of Timor the *I-121* claims to have sunk a Dutch freighter, which they identified as the *Bantamu*, of 9312 tons. However, Dutch records state otherwise – the ship, actually the *Bantam* – survived the war.

The rationale behind deploying the submarine squadron so far south deserves some consideration. At the time the Japanese military advance was successfully sweeping all before them: they had seized Kuala Lumpur on 11 January and also taken the island of Tarakan. Their drive further south was already planned: Balikpapan and Rabaul were to be targets a little while later. This would bring them the vital assets of the Netherlands East Indies' supplies of oil and rubber. However, the possibility of a counterstrike from Darwin must have been on their minds too, and the successful mining of the harbour would have slowed delivery to the port of resources, which were delivered almost entirely by sea. Once the first mines were encountered, either by sweeping, sighting or contact, the free passage of ships would be dramatically slowed, with shipping channels needing constant attention, a requirement for which many corvettes would be needed, with long and careful minesweeping holding up the convoys. The definite sighting of submarines would be a similar damper on shipping activity. At this time shipping via the Torres Strait was heavier than ever, as the main supply route from the USA to the NEI or the Philippines was via Torres Strait. Many of these ships put into Darwin for supplies or to get new orders given the rapidly changing situation. The submarines therefore were sent on a daring mission, but one which if successful would strike an essential blow.

On 10 January *I-124* left port for southern waters together with *I-123*. On 14 January the submarines sighted the American cruiser *Houston* and two destroyers and tracked them towards Darwin, but missed an opportunity for attack. The *Houston* reported sighting a periscope, and left *Edsall* searching unsuccessfully in the area. On 16 January *I-124* laid 27 mines, probably to the south of Bathurst Island. *I-123* meanwhile had changed course off the Coburg Peninsula and made her way west towards *I-124*'s patrol area. According to a Japanese monograph and

The submarine squadron's track southwards. The separate tracks of each boat can be identified at first in the north, with the name of each boat alongside its track. The strategic plan here is simple but effective – with a combination of mines and the submarine's torpedoes the squadron could contain ships in Darwin's harbour, and also deter others from approaching. The potency of the submarine weapon is readily apparent. Four relatively lightly-armed warships, by a combination of weapons and the mere possibility of their presence – the numbers of boats and location of the squadron are in theory unknown to the enemy – could paralyse a port. (National Institute for Defence Studies, Japan.)

A mine floating outside Darwin Harbour (the ships in the background might be the two gate ships of the boom). Hitting such a mine – very difficult to see in the daytime and impossible to see at night – would mean the end for many types of small ship such as the Bathurst-class corvette. Several mines from the submarine squadron were located over the next few months after I-124's sinking. (E. Woodward collection/NT Library).

maps *I-122* had taken up station outside the Melville Island and Coburg Peninsula gap; *I-121* had been ordered to reverse course to take up station outside Darwin, but whether she did or not is unclear.

However, it seems certain that on 19 January there were at least three submarines waiting outside Darwin, doubtless drawn to a target that promised at least one cruiser as well as concentrations of merchant shipping. The mined routes into Darwin were now a lethal trap for unwary ships, and to add to the threat the submarine squadron was lying in wait, armed with torpedoes and deck guns.

Of especial interest is the fact that the Americans knew with certainty there were submarines in the area. Added to the *Houston* group's reported sighting was Japanese radio intelligence deciphered by American teams and passed on to Australian Naval Intelligence. Barbara Winter, in *The Intrigue Master*, explains how this was done: the Americans were deciphering the messages of the Japanese Commander of the Southern Area Subforce, who on the 19th reported that: "*I-124* is approaching Darwin Harbor mouth".

Mines are a potent weapon in warfare, and the mere threat of mines having been laid will force the potential victim to sweep and search, investigate every suspicious underwater object, and in general conduct every operation, from convoy escort to anti-submarine patrol, with a lot more care, and therefore, time, money and effort spent. In short, the submarine squadron operations carried the potential with it to temporarily paralyse operations into Darwin's port and the waters around northern Australia.

Meanwhile the assembled forces designed to deal with such a threat were gathering strength in Australia's Top End. According to Alan Powell's authoritative account of war in the north, *The Shadow's Edge*, the 24th Minesweeping Flotilla, composed of Australian corvettes, was moved to Darwin at the end of 1941. Seven of the vessels sailed north over a period of two months, amongst them *HMAS Deloraine*.

Strategically speaking, Squadron Commander Endo on board *I-124* had made a good decision. He had laid mine fields to sink ships, and a glance at the map depicting the squadron's deployment outside Darwin illustrates how the mines and waiting submarines were to be used. Ships sighting any loose mines would be driven towards the submarines; ships hearing or sighting the submarines and changing course to avoid them would be driven towards the minefields. The only flaw in the plan was the shallow depth of water in which the submarines were forced to wait. But Endo's dilemma only had one possible outcome for success: if the submarines waited in deeper water the possibilities for ships to avoid them would increase tremendously as they would have many different courses to choose from. So, bravely, the submarine captains chose the certainty of combat over the possibility of avoidance – and failure.

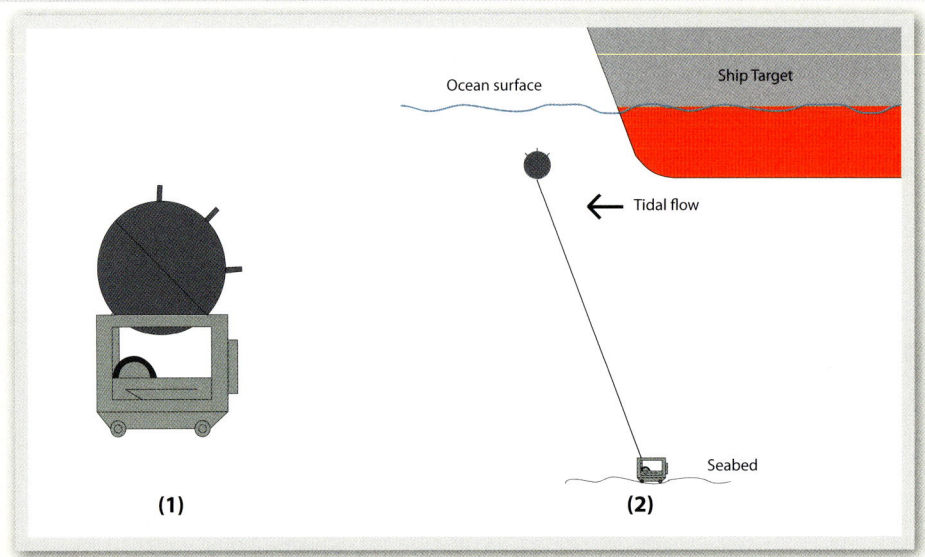

JAPANESE TYPE 88 SUBMARINE MINE

(1) A stowed mine. This diagram was drawn with reference to a British submarine mine, but it is understood the Japanese Type 88 mine, as employed by I-124, shared the same design principles. Seen here is the mine in stowed position, sitting on top of a sinker-box which also contained a cable winch. The assembly sat on roller wheels and was ejected from the submarine by a rail system.

(2) A deployed mine. The sinker-box acts as an anchor on the ocean floor. The mine itself is connected by a cable, which unrolls until a hydrostatic mechanism floats the mine at a pre-set depth, so the position, although not depth, of the mine would vary with the tidal flow. The mine would explode when a vessel contacts any of the mine "horns". In the waters near Darwin the tidal forces were so great that the entire assembly, or broken portions of it, were washed ashore or out to sea. None of the mines laid by Japanese submarines caused any damage.

Graphic by Peter Ingman

CHAPTER 5

– COMBAT LEADERS

What sort of men led the two ships that were shortly to meet in combat? Lieutenant Commander Desmond Menlove had been a man of the sea for many years before he joined *Deloraine* in 1941. He was born in Temora, NSW in 1906, the youngest of the three children of a bank manager with the Bank of NSW. Entering the Royal Australian Navy in 1920 in his 14th year, the young boy's full-time naval career at first was a brief one. He trained at the RAN College in Jervis Bay, and in 1921 became a midshipman.

Later, with the Defence cuts of the 1920s, Menlove was transferred to the Reserve, and subsequently joined the Merchant Navy, first serving in the Australian Commonwealth Line. He then worked for the Canadian-Australasian Royal Mail Line, the premier trans-Pacific link from Sydney to Vancouver, and later the Union Steamship Company. In 1938 he joined the Eastern Australian Steamship Company, which plied mainly between Australia and Eastern ports such as Hong Kong and various Japanese destinations. Colleague William Craike, who served with him in those days, remembers him as "a keen and efficient officer....who did not suffer fools gladly". While Menlove rose steadily through the ranks of the Merchant service, his Reserve training continued on a regular basis, with eventual promotion to Lieutenant.

In 1936 Menlove married Marion Stevens, daughter of a retired RAN Captain. In 1939 they had a son, Warwick, born while Desmond was in Yokohama. In June 1939 the Naval Board announced a general mobilisation of the RAN Reserve. Moving the family to Sydney, Menlove joined the light cruiser *HMAS Adelaide* as a watchkeeping officer. He was promoted to Lieutenant Commander in 1940, and became the Navigator of *Adelaide*, serving on board during the incident when the ship's presence helped prevent an attempted Vichy coup in New Caledonia in September 1940.

The rest of *Deloraine*'s crew was made up from a myriad of men with an enormous variation in experience. Some were civilian volunteers: bank clerks, stockmen, tradesmen with a variety of skills that could be useful in a warship, those of electricians, mechanics, fitters and turners. Many had been members of the Navy's Reserve, and therefore had received naval training

Desmond Menlove at sea in the 1920s (Jean Menlove)

over a number of years. British-born officer Lieutenant Eric Thompson, for example, had joined the RAN in 1936 in Hobart, and had seen service with the Royal Navy before being posted to *Deloraine*, where he was the Gunnery Officer. Other crew members stayed with *Deloraine* for the entire war: Arthur Waller, for example, was present at the commissioning ceremony in 1941 as a Petty Officer Stoker, and was the last of the steaming crew to leave the ship in 1945 as a Chief Petty Officer.

The commander of *I-124*, by contrast to *Deloraine*'s captain, had spent all of his working life in the Imperial Japanese Navy. Lieutenant Commander Kouichi Kishigami had been a naval officer since his induction into the Academy of the Imperial Japanese Navy three days after his 17th birthday, on 26 August, 1921. He graduated as a member of the 52nd class nearly three years later on 24 July, 1924.

Kishigami's naval career saw him posted to a number of submarine squadrons: the 1st Squadron in 1932 and the 2nd Squadron in 1937. He also served at the Kure Naval Station for a number of years prior to the 2nd Squadron engagement. Promotion was steady: from Ensign to Sub-Lieutenant in 1925; to Lieutenant in 1931, and finally to Lieutenant Commander in 1937. In contrast to some Allied naval officers, Kishigami spent all of his service in a single branch of his navy, specifically submarines, and it was probably a measure of his expertise that he was appointed a submarine school instructor in 1938. By then he would have been expecting promotion to full commander and the coveted "brass-hat": the gold leaf that adorns the cap of this rank of naval officer and those above, the equivalent of the army's lieutenant-colonel, and a sign that the wearer may be destined for greater heights. It is not unreasonable to assume that given *I-124*'s successful start to her wartime career, that Kishigami would have received this promotion on his return from the squadron's sortie south.

Kishigami's wife Fusae accompanied him on his various postings in the Imperial Japanese Navy of the 1920s and 1930s. The family of four, including the two daughters Atsuko and Etsuko, were based for a time at Kure in the prefecture of Nagasaki, where Kishigami was a teacher in the Navy's submarine school. In 1941 he received his last posting – to command *I-124* under the supervision of Squadron Commander Endo.

Atsuko Kishigami remembers her father only a little. "I was 12 when the news came of his loss", she says. However, she remembers the family together before the war, and her father's navy uniform, with its two-and-a-half stripes on the shoulders. In his moments of relaxation, she remembers, Kouichi played the shakuhachi, a musical instrument rather like the flute. When he left for *I-124*'s final voyage, he was 37.

Commander Keiyu Endo, the Squadron Commander, was 46 years old at the time of *I-124*'s mission to Australia. Supervising all four boats, he chose to embark in *I-124*, a decision that would cost him his life. Born in 1896, Endo had a largely uneventful career. His son Kenji remembers being told by a naval cabin-boy that Commander Endo was a gentle man by comparison with many other naval officers: in the Imperial Japanese Navy physical punishment of sailors by officers was not illegal and not uncommon. Endo had a long career in the navy: he had commanded a submarine tender and a submarine base, and left behind a wife, Hisa, and Mieko, a daughter, as well as his son Kenji. His promotion to Captain was confirmed after *I-124* failed to return, as was Kishigami's to Commander.

One of Menlove's early ships, TSS Awatea, passing Sydney Harbour Bridge in 1936. (Jean Menlove)

The Kishigami family (l/r): Lieutenant Commander Kouichi Kishigami, daughters Atsuko and Etsuko, and wife Fusae. (Atsuko Kishigami)

The then-Lieutenant Desmond Menlove (left) on board HMAS Adelaide, August 1940, with (l/r) Surgeon Commander Hasker and Paymaster Commander White. (Jean Menlove)

CHAPTER 6

– BATTLE!

There are several accounts of *I-124*'s sinking but one of the reasons this book was written is that some are inaccurate, and others are biased. Theodore Roscoe's *United States Destroyer Operations in World War II*, for example, gives the credit for the victory equally to *USS Edsall* and *HMAS Deloraine*: "...destroyer *Edsall* and corvette *Deloraine* could each paint a Rising Sun naval flag on the ship's "scoreboard." [1] Others are even more contradictory. *The Dictionary of American Naval Fighting Ships*, says

> "With three Australian corvettes, *Edsall* sent *I-124* to the bottom on 20 January 1942 off Darwin." WG Winslow in *The Fleet the Gods Forgot* simply gives full credit to *Edsall* for the sinking.[2] The official Australian naval history goes further and shares it between *Edsall* and two more corvettes: *Lithgow* and *Katoomba*. But what actually happened?

ATTACK ON A CONVOY...ON BOARD *USS TRINITY*

The principal ship of a Darwin-bound convoy, *USS Trinity* was a fleet oiler, and was at 5, 375 tons a high-value target in a war theatre. Having recently left Koepang Bay under the escort of two destroyers, *USS Whipple* and *USS John D. Edwards*, on the morning of 20 January 1942, *Trinity* had successfully and safely steamed through the Timor Sea and was now nearly at her destination of Darwin. The voyage had been quite peaceful, although busy: *Trinity* had met and refueled over a dozen ships; had met and exchanged recognition signals with a Lockheed Hudson aircraft, and had mistakenly gone to General Quarters when what was supposed to be a flare was sighted; later thought to have been a meteorite. *Trinity* had also exchanged her original escorting destroyers for the two that were now her anti-submarine screen, *USS Edsall* and *USS Alden*.

Waiting in the convoy's path was a formidable combination of minefields and the minelaying submarines. Commander Endo had planned his strategy well. Minefields had been laid in pre-planned areas, and outside this unseen menace he had allocated his submarines a patrol area

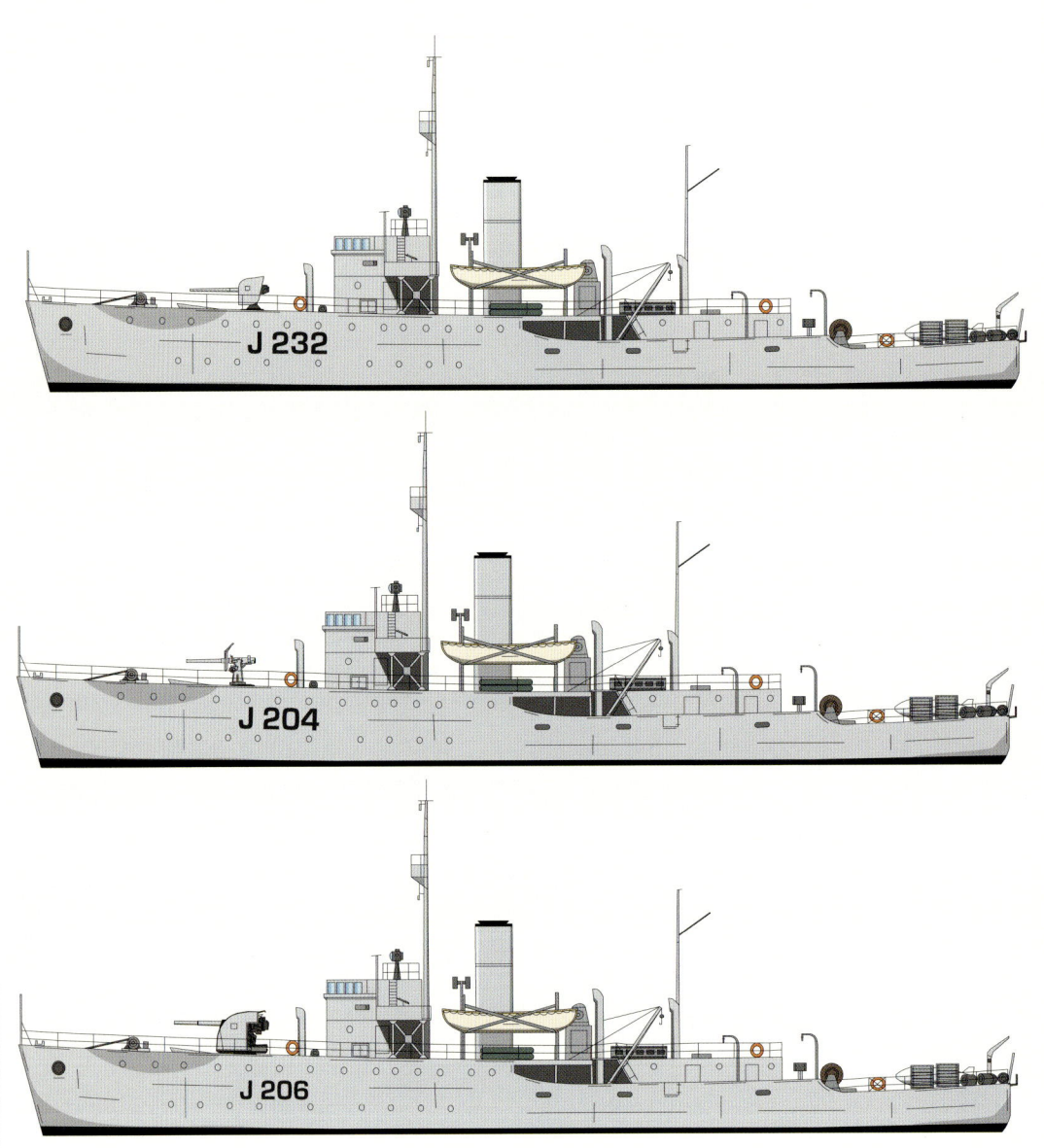

The three RAN corvettes of the 24th M/S Flotilla based in Darwin in January 1942. HMAS Lithgow, lower, had been commissioned in mid-1941 and received a new 4-inch gun as was intended for the design. However, both HMAS Katoomba (middle) and HMAS Deloraine (top) were commissioned in late 1941. By this time the new 4-inch guns were not available and both entered service with different types of old 12-pounder (3-inch) guns. All were newly arrived in Darwin when called to fight I-124, indeed Lithgow and Katoomba had only been in the northern port for one day after escorting American merchant ships from Thursday Island.

Graphic by Peter Ingman

each. Endo had every reason to anticipate success. Into the trap came the American convoy. According to the squadron's records, *I-123*, under the command of Lieutenant Commander Ueno, was the first submarine to attack, using a spread of four torpedoes.

Lieutenant George E. Marix was in command of *Trinity*'s bridge as "Officer of the Deck" when the *I-123* attacked. He subsequently reported he was standing on the port bridge wing in the early dawn, talking to the Captain, when the first report of a torpedo was made at approximately 0620:

> I heard the control officer, Ensign Tothero, call out "Torpedo wake to starboard, parallel." I ran through the wheel house and in passing ordered the helmsman to hold his course. As I reached the starboard wing of the bridge I saw the wake of a torpedo passing from astern and running parallel to the ship. The torpedo passed about 25 feet from the side.

The torpedo wake was also seen by Yeoman 1st Class T.F. Drag, who described it as "highly phosphorescent", although this seems strange, in what by then was daylight. *Trinity*'s captain immediately ordered a course change and full speed. A crewman readied the signaling pistol, and the prearranged message of a white Very light was fired to indicate a torpedo had been sighted. "General quarters" was sounded, and immediately signals were made by light to the escorting destroyers to indicate the course of the sighted torpedo. A few minutes later another torpedo wake was sighted, again by Ensign Tothero; this second attack also coming from astern and missing this time by a bigger margin: some "75 to 100 yards" according to the Ensign. The course was changed yet again, and two minutes later a third torpedo was seen, this time sighted by several people on the bridge. A few moments later in the distance the double explosion of two depth charges was both seen and heard: the escorting destroyer *Alden* had gained a sonar contact and was attacking.

Meanwhile *Trinity* was still at her full speed, with *Edsall* ahead of her and *Alden* left behind. At 0700 land was sighted; a little while later *Alden* rejoined the convoy, and at 0950 *Deloraine* was sighted on her patrolling station outside the harbour. The convoy was now in the defended "swept channel" actively patrolled by RAN corvettes. Soon the boom gate was opened for the American ships and they passed into the relative safety of Darwin Harbour. At 1220 *Trinity* was at anchor in the busy Darwin harbour, having joined over 20 Australian and American ships. Her news, that she had survived a multiple torpedo attack, would surely have been of immense importance to the captains of these other ships: it now meant that the boom-netted harbour was only a temporary refuge and each departing ship would have to run the gauntlet of submarines possibly lurking outside the harbour entrance.

DELORAINE'S FIGHT

At 1155 on the 20th of January *Deloraine* was conducting minesweeping operations outside Darwin harbour, when she received a wireless message from naval command. In Fleet Code the ship was given a Priority "O" signal. Bill Hornery remembers:

> Duty WT operator sent for me. Half way through decoding I called for the CO to come to the voicepipe - orally gave him the purport of the signal to date. CO ordered to cease sweeping. CO pulled the completed message up the voicepipe and *Deloraine* proceeded with speed.

She was to proceed immediately to the scene of the attack on the convoy, where she would receive support from a US aircraft. Equipped with modern ASDIC domes under their hulls, the Australian corvettes were well equipped to hunt underwater targets once the general location was known (reliable detection ranges were usually within 2, 000 yards). They also presented small and difficult targets for torpedo attacks.

At 14 knots *Deloraine* headed on a course of 275° towards the action. She was to get more than she bargained for. At 1335 Lieutenant Commander Menlove moved out onto the starboard bridge wing to view an aircraft which had just been sighted. As he did so, the starboard lookout, Able Seaman O'Neill, sighted a torpedo and immediately called out, as did Petty Officer Arthur Waller, who was some distance away on the upper deck midships. This was reported as "Torpedo approaching Green 100", which means that the torpedo was on *Deloraine*'s starboard/right side

USS Trinity in 1938 whilst undergoing preparation for active service. Probably taken at the Philadelphia Navy Yard. (US Naval Historical Centre)

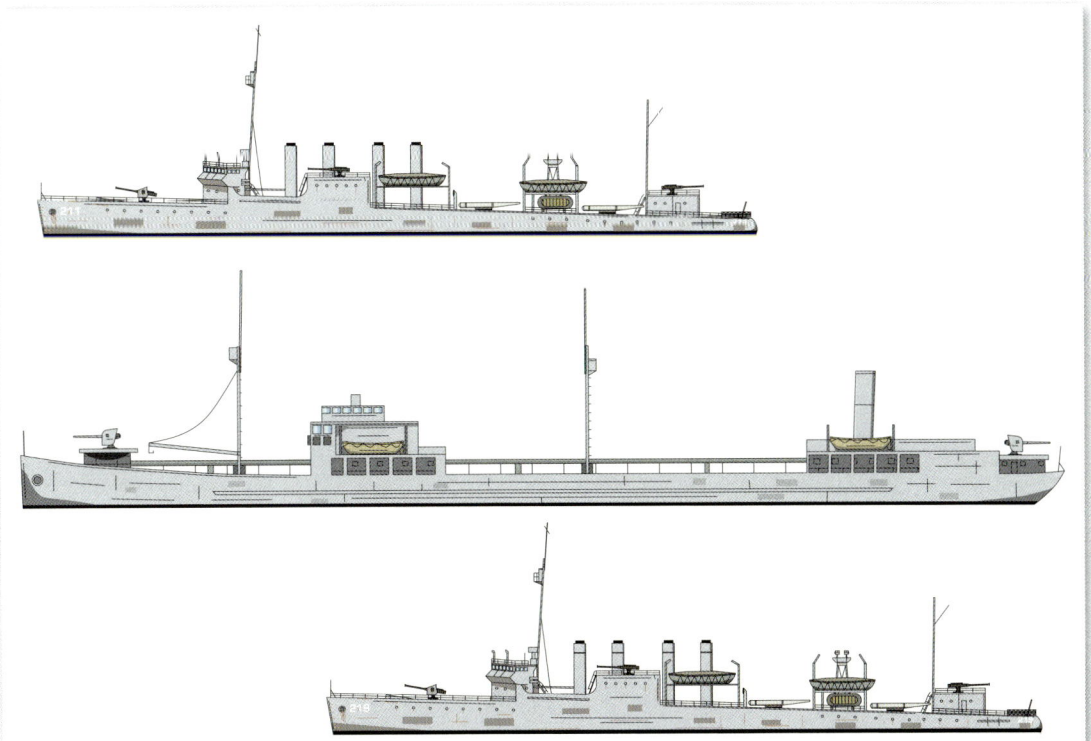

Oiler USS Trinity, centre, with escorting destroyers USS Alden and USS Edsall. These were the ships that narrowly escaped the trap set by the Japanese mine-laying submarines off Darwin in January 1942. While drawn to scale, from this view it is not immediately clear how "fat" a target was Trinity. While the destroyers had a beam of 31 feet and a draught of nine feet, the oiler had a beam of 60 feet and a draught of 26 feet – a vastly larger target. After avoiding torpedoes from I-123, the convoy hurried into the relative safety of Darwin Harbour. RAN corvettes were sent out to hunt the submarines. The US destroyers later returned to the scene to provide back-up for the corvettes: the destroyers could out-run and out-gun a surfaced submarine, unlike the corvettes.

Graphic by Peter Ingman

at 100 degrees, assuming the ship's bow as zero. Lieutenant Commander Menlove's response was immediate. He ordered the ship to turn to starboard, so she was swinging to present her bow to the torpedo, thereby presenting a much smaller target, and increased to full power to cause the torpedo to miss. His decision was the right one – the torpedo passed ten feet behind *Deloraine*'s stern; wireman Stan Hale, sitting on a bollard, saw the wake and ran to the stern, where he "...saw the wake of torpedo virtually pass under the counter". Frank Marsh also attests to the close call:

> I was on board *Deloraine* and saw the trail of the torpedo which missed our stern so close that the wake thrown up by the propellers actually caused the torpedo to come out of the raised sea surface. I was off watch and on the forward deck at the time of the sighting and have long savoured the corvette's manoeuvrability and Captain Menlove's skill.

5819-42 (DD211).
STERN VIEW.
ALTERATIONS CIRCLED ON M.I. PHOTOS NOS.
5807-42, 5809-42, 5810-42.
MARE ISLAND. CAL. SEPTEMBER 22, 1942.

USS Alden off the Mare Island Navy Yard, 22 September 1942. (US Naval Historical Centre)

Deloraine closed up to action stations and was quickly in sonar contact with the submarine, now dead ahead. As the corvette raced up the torpedo's wake Stan Hale, busy with depth charges on the stern's quarterdeck, thinks he and Fred Savage saw a periscope: "...about 30 ft. away in line with the port thrower....we saw it turn towards us. When it focussed on the ship the periscope started to go down just as the buzzer sounded to drop a depth charge."

Three planes were circling over the spot, according to Menlove's report, one Catalina, almost certainly from the locally-based American Patrol Wing 10, and two "American float planes". Eight minutes after the torpedo attack *Deloraine* carried out her first depth charge run. Two of the bombs were hurled into the air by her port and starboard throwers, and four launched by rail on both sides of the ship. Frank Marsh at this stage reports that one of the American planes dropped "a small bomb". From this onslaught both oil and air bubbles were seen breaking the surface, and the ship was put onto a reciprocal heading to repeat the attack.

A second series of depth charges was launched, and then the submarine broke the surface. Menlove reports her at 1349 as showing both her periscope and bow, and he had time to note a five degree trim by the stern and a list of at least twenty degrees to port. The periscope he describes as black, and the submarine itself a "rusty colour". He also says, in a later account of the action, "I 124 on the conning tower". Frank Marsh also saw the periscope: "it turned its hood to face us then promptly dived." W. Eric Thompson, the Gunnery Lieutenant, remembers:

...after the first pattern of depth charges had detonated...I was attempting to calculate a range should we be involved in a gun duel. Emerging from the erupting swirling waters I could see something oval shaped and black; before I could properly determine what part of the enemy I was seeing, the float plane dropped its bomb almost on top of the submarine. *Deloraine* was turning towards, under 30° of helm, one was grabbing for support on the heeling bridge and the sea was boiling and discoloured from the explosion of the bomb.

Menlove was altering the ship's course so the port depth charge thrower, manned by Leading Seaman Fred Savage, could bear and this was immediately fired; the charge observed to land no fewer than ten feet from the submarine's periscope. Menlove reported the aircraft attack bomb landing almost at the same spot as the depth charge, and Lieutenant Thompson identified it as "a Vought Sikorsky seaplane from *USS Langley*"[3] which was berthed in Darwin at the time. These were a small USN catapult-launched plane known as a "Kingfisher".[a]

After these explosions the submarine's sonar signal was reported as steady. With no Doppler[b] effect observed the target was judged to be stationary on the seabed. Oil and air bubbles were seen in "very large quantities". At 1356 another attack was ordered with six depth charges. More bubbles were seen, and *Deloraine* was slowed to make closer observations. Oil was collected in buckets, and "particles of T.N.T. were also observed". *Deloraine*, her radio having become faulty early in the attack sequence, used flashing light to report her attack and findings to the circling Catalina overhead.

At half past two in the afternoon (1430) *Deloraine* gained another sonar contact. This one was off to the south-east at 3000 yards. Some ten minutes later *Deloraine* launched two of the last five of her depth charges. More oil and air was seen to rise, and this attack was followed by another with the last three depth charges. [c]

At 1500 *Deloraine* reported her ammunition state, but stayed in the area to help with the submarine's prosecution. For some time she acted as "directing vessel" for *Lithgow*, and at 1748, with the arrival of *Katoomba* – whose commander outranked Menlove – *Deloraine* was ordered

---

a   The official designation was OS2U; three variants were known, with a 1, 2 or 3 following the official type number. Powered by a single engine, the plane seated two, and mounted a forward-firing machine gun and one ring-mounted "flexible" machine gun, and also carried two bombs, apparently ranging from 100 to 325 pounds.

b   Doppler, used to determine a submariner's movement and direction, refers to the difference in pitch a sound makes according to whether it is moving in relation to the listener, or if the listener is moving in relation to a stationary object. A train whistle, for example, seems to change in pitch as the train draws near to you while standing on a platform, and then appears to change in pitch as it passes and moves away. In fact, the pitch is the same at all times.

c   As she was carrying bulky minesweeping gear, *Deloraine* could only embark around 20 depth charges. These were Mk VII Depth Charges, with a total weight of around 420 pounds each. A short time later *Deloraine* reported embarking a standard outfit of 35 depth charges, presumably without her minesweeping gear. Source: Reports of Proceedings HMAS Deloraine, 1942. AWM78 97/1.

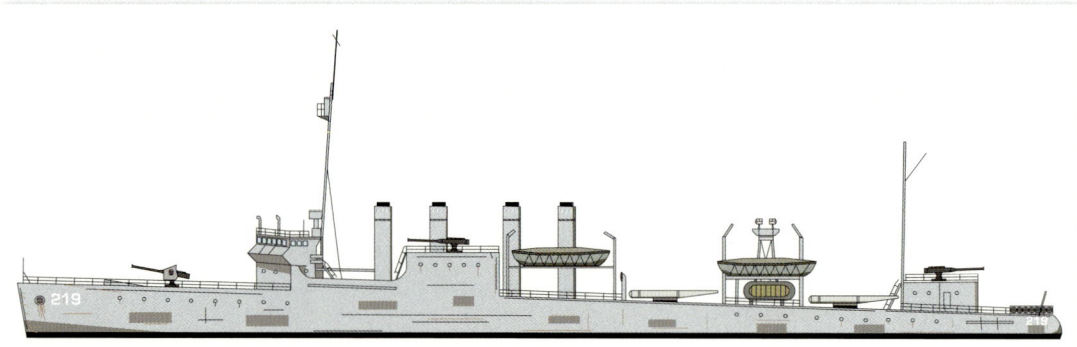

USS EDSALL DD-219

Type: *Clemson-class destroyer*   **Commissioned:** *1920*

Displacement: *1,190 tons*   **Length:** *314'5 feet*   **Beam:** *31'9 feet*

Maximum Speed: *35 knots*   **Complement:** *101*

Armament: *4 x 4-inch guns; 12 x 21-inch Torpedo Tubes; Machine Guns; Depth Charges*

USS Edsall (DD-219) and USS Alden (DD-211) were Clemson-class destroyers, part of a massive naval building program put in place towards the end of WWI. Known as "flush deckers" or "four pipers", this class gave the USN the largest destroyer fleet in the world. Although successfully mass-produced, the design had shortcomings. For example, the ships were notably "wet" and the forward gun could not be used in a head sea. In the mid-1930s they were obsolete as destroyers, and many were converted into seaplane tenders, fast transports or minesweepers. At the start of the Pacific War the only "flush deckers" still serving as front-line destroyers were those with the Asiatic Fleet in Manila. Many of these ships visited Darwin during January 1942. Their WWI-era sensors meant they were relatively poor submarine hunters, although their speed and armament made them deadly adversaries for surfaced submarines.   Graphic by Peter Ingman

back to Darwin to meet the local patrol vessel *Vigilant* and re-arm.[d] The two ships met off Charles Point, just outside Darwin's harbour entrance, and frantic loading of depth charges took place with the ships alongside each other – Stan Hale recalls fitting the pistols to the depth charges' detonators in the dark. After 15 depth charges had been loaded *Deloraine* set off to rendezvous with *Katoomba*.

At five past three that morning *Deloraine* obtained another submarine echo. Action stations was duly sounded. At 0321 the ship passed a dan buoy which had been laid the previous afternoon to mark the position of the presumed submarine, and along with it a large oil patch, presumably from an enemy below. A minute later two patterns of two depth charges were dropped. The oil patch was now reported to have increased in size, and "a very strong smell of oil was noticeable". Two more charges were soon thrown – *Deloraine*'s report does not specify the exact time. From then on until 1155 that morning Menlove's command came under the direction of *Katoomba*, and both ships dropped more depth charges.

---

d   HMAS *Vigilant* was a former Department of Trade and Customs vessel of 106 tons requisitioned in 1940. She arrived in Darwin in mid-1941 and had been used on the Darwin-Timor run. *Vigilant* was under the command of Sub-Lieutenant HA Bennett, RANR, who captained the vessel until the end of 1943. (Details courtesy Gill)

Around midday on the 21st all of the ships called off the attack; with the weather deteriorating and the submarine contact stationary the action was judged to be over. Soon *Deloraine* was guarding the boom vessel *Kookaburra* as she commenced diving operations. The story of *I-124* was about to enter a new chapter.

On Board *I-124?*

We will never certainly know, unless *I-124*'s log book is ever recovered, how the day's events unfolded on board the submarine. We can gather that *I-124* fired at least one torpedo towards *Deloraine*. Lieutenant Commander Kishigami would have had his fire-control team set up a firing solution for the speeding corvette, having probably sighted the ship's mast some considerable time previously. Whether it was known that a warship was approaching is unknown, but the crew would have suspected as much; given that morning's attack on the *Trinity* convoy, which *I-124* may have known of; it is possible that Squadron Commander Endo communicated with his squadron. Perhaps *I-124* herself had made an abortive attack on the convoy, or heard her sister's ship attack and the subsequent depth-charging. At any rate, the submarine commanders were all on the lookout for possible targets, and now Kishigami was to have his chance.

Kishigami's fire-solution would have been set up by his own crew, with the Squadron Commander and his staff looking on; this much we can surmise given Endo's character and the universal naval tradition of a Flag Officer allowing his flagship captain to run his own ship. *Deloraine* was steaming towards a spot where the fired torpedoes and the corvette would intercept: the calculation had to allow for the warship's course and speed; the speed of the torpedo; tidal movements...a complicated affair, and a calculation that in hindsight we can see that Kishigami got completely correct. If it was not for bridge lookout Able Seaman O'Neill's attention to duty; Lieutenant Commander Menlove's quick and correct response and the immediate obeying of the engine-room orders – if not for *Deloraine* functioning as an efficient warship with a united crew – then it would certainly have been *Deloraine* that settled on the seabed on that day.

The response to the miss on the submarine would have been immense disappointment, quickly replaced by the knowledge that now the hunter would become the hunted. As *Deloraine* charged down the torpedo bearing the instinctive response would have been to go deep – difficult in the shallow depth of a few hundred feet beneath the boat – and to run silently. Kishigami's best chance lay in avoiding detection, because once he was found, the shallow waters and restrictive shores around him would greatly inhibit his escape. The immediate detonation of *Deloraine*'s depth charges would have been shattering – equipment would have been torn from

A RAAF Catalina in Darwin later in the war. These aircraft were big, twin-engined, long range aircraft which were used in a variety of missions by Allied forces around the world. Seven were lost in Darwin Harbour during the war – the wrecks remain in a variety of states and are regularly visited by scuba divers. (NT Library)

bulkheads; the boat would have been shaken violently; there may have been partial power loss in sections of the boat; possible injuries; perhaps even some water leaks into the boat. As the depth charging continued the crew would have been able to hear *Deloraine*'s engines overhead, growing and fading as the corvette wheeled around her target. And always there would have been the relentless pinging of the corvette's sonar.

Perhaps, as the depth charging continued, Kishigami decided to take a chance. He may have presumed that he was fighting one ship, and he probably knew from the propellers' sound that it was a small ship, a small destroyer or corvette. Perhaps therefore he decided to surface in the knowledge that his 5.5 inch gun would outweigh the armament of such a ship, and if he were lucky, then he could open fire and hold off the warship, meanwhile taking advantage of the boat's surface speed – far greater than the underwater speed, and comparable to the corvette's – to escape.[e]

However, one look through the periscope as the submarine neared the surface may have

---

e   Writing of his experiences in WWII submarines, Vice Admiral Sir Hugh Mackenzie recalls in his book *The Sword of Damocles* that the RN submarine crews were well versed in the use of their deck guns: "....from periscope depth to opening fire on the surface a good time was twenty to twenty-five seconds, rate of fire was of the order of seventeen rounds per minute, from which ten hits should be achieved on a target measuring twenty feet by ten feet at a range of one thousand yards". (p. 48-49) convinced Kishigami of the folly of such an action. He would have indeed seen a small warship, but he would also have perhaps seen others approaching – or their masts – and perhaps he saw the circling aircraft as well. Perhaps, however, the depth-charging had damaged a ballast tank, and *I-124* came to the surface accidentally. Maybe she fired another torpedo or more – although none was seen – and the design faults of the minelayers caused the bow to rise too suddenly. Whatever the case, it was then that the decisive blow was struck in the battle: an aircraft's small ineffective bomb was joined by the thunderous discharge of one of *Deloraine*'s quarter-ton depth charges. The submarine was sent plunging to the seabed, where it probably struck the bottom with a final crash, causing even more damage.

Desperate attempts at movement would have then followed. In the divers' reports, made some days afterwards, there is some evidence that *I-124* moved once she was on the bottom. Such movement may well have brought further depth charging. *I-124* was certainly crippled, however, and the crew's attempts to manoeuvre or bring the submarine to the surface were fruitless. Some of them would already be injured, but soon the injuries would not matter. They were trapped.

HMAS Deloraine undergoing a re-paint, perhaps in Darwin. (Royal Australian Navy)

THE COMPANION SHIPS' STORIES: ON BOARD *LITHGOW*

HMAS Lithgow, another *Bathurst* class corvette, had also been at anchor in Darwin harbour that morning, but not for long. The unsuccessful action against the convoy must be met with a swift and stern response. Laid down in 1940, and having completed her fitting out in mid-1941, *Lithgow* had helped escort a convoy, arriving in port on the 19 January; the group of ships incidentally containing the American transports *USAT Meigs* and *USAT Mauna Loa*, to be sunk a month later within the harbour by the Japanese carrier group which wreaked such havoc within Darwin.

In January 1942 *Lithgow* was under the command of Commander AV Knight, RANR(S). Like the other two corvette commanders, Knight was a member of the Royal Australian Navy's Reserve. An Englishman born in 1897, Knight was the oldest of the commanding officers on the scene.

On Tuesday 20 January *Lithgow* was ordered by Darwin's Naval Officer in Charge – Captain EP Thomas, RN – to proceed from Darwin harbour to sea at full speed. Leaving Darwin at 1328, over two hours later at 1615 *Deloraine* was sighted. *Lithgow*'s first attack on a possible submarine contact was carried out at 1710 with a pattern of six depth charges. Following another attack she reported "bubbles of oil and air". The third attack was even more successful: "very heavy oil and much air and it appeared that the submarine almost surfaced..." Altogether *Lithgow* carried out seven attacks, expending all of her 40 depth charges, and at 1839 she was ordered back to Darwin by *Katoomba*, passing through the boom at 2236.

An hour later *Lithgow* again proceeded to sea – her report does not hint at the frantic efforts that must have been undertaken to rearm and refuel her. At daylight on 21 Wednesday she again reached the combat area. This time she contacted *Katoomba* as well as *Deloraine*, and at 0905 reported circling in thick oil "rising from a position to the East South East of the submarine destroyed the previous afternoon." The other two ships attacked and *Lithgow* eventually "pointed" to the position of the submarine for the boom vessel *Kookaburra*, which had arrived on the scene. *Lithgow* also provided anti-submarine cover for the boom vessel, which was to be the platform for diving on the sunken submarine.

Over the next few days *Lithgow* returned to the busy life of a hard-working maid of all work – a glance at her reports for the next few days gives a picture of just how difficult the corvette sailor's life was. She searched for a possible submarine reported by *Alden*; she towed *Katoomba* back to port after that ship had a major collision with the tanker *USS Pecos*; she investigated a report of a second submarine five miles from the now marked site of the first submarine sinking, and on the 25th joined yet another search resulting from a real or imagined submarine contact.

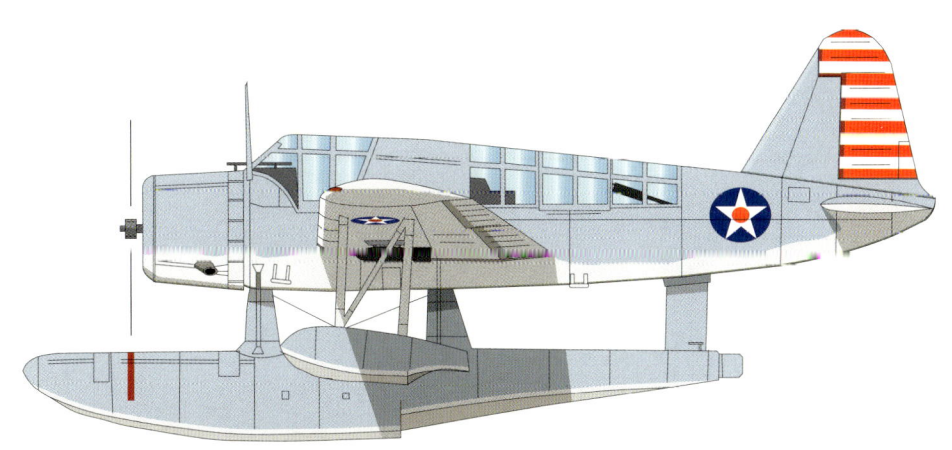

TYPE: OS2U KINGFISHER AIRCRAFT 2-SEAT OBSERVATION FLOATPLANE

*1 x 450 hp radial engine   **Max speed:** 175 mph   **Cruising speed:** 119 mph   **Range:** 900 miles*
***Armament:** 1 x forward firing 0.30-inch MG; 1 x aft-firing 0.30-inch MG on flexible mount; 2 x 100-lb underwing bombs*

The Kingfisher was the most widely produced floatplane of WWII, replacing biplane types in United States Naval service. A few were serving with Patrol Wing 10 (which was primarily equipped with long-range PBY Catalinas), in the Philippines in December 1941. The ex-carrier USS Langley was used as a base-ship by this unit. Being too large and unwieldy for front-line operations, Langley was sent to Darwin. One PatWing10 OS2U Kingfisher floatplane remained with Langley and flew local anti-submarine patrols during January 1942. This aircraft assisted Deloraine in detecting and sinking I-124 and was seen to drop a bomb on the submerged submarine. However the bombs carried at that time were relatively small (less than a quarter the size of a depth charge) and were probably ineffective against an underwater target.
Interestingly, US sources do not mention the role of this aircraft during the incident. However, Langley was sunk the following month, taking both records and possibly some of the personnel involved with her (the aircraft itself had been transferred to USS Heron before Langley departed Darwin). A better-documented combat involving Kingfishers co-operating with the New Zealand corvette HMNZS Tui occurred on 19 August 1943 off Noumea. By this time the Kingfishers, from Scouting Squadron VS-57, were equipped with underwing depth charges, and these sank submarine I-17.

Graphic by Peter Ingman

USS EDSALL

As outlined above, and quite strangely in the light of inspection, this destroyer is credited in quite a few reports as having helped in the sinking of *I-124*. An examination of the commander's report does not support this, and indeed, there are no contemporary reports of the *Edsall* being involved in the submarine's destruction. Crew members in *Deloraine* do not recall seeing the US ship at the action; as Bill Hornery explains: "...there were only four corvettes finally present at the scene but *Deloraine* was the only one at the kill. It was some time later that we were reinforced. I have never heard of *Edsall* being there."

Some of Deloraine's crew on the quarterdeck: (l/r) Stan Hale, in white shorts; AB Richard Holder; with arm raised PO Andy Hook; seated LS Ken Crannage. The depth charges are the large drums port and starboard; the large torpedo-like objects are called "French Floats", part of the minesweeping gear. (Stan Hale)

The *Edsall*'s commander, Lieutenant Joshua J. Nix, first reported entering the action against a submarine during the attack on the convoy on the morning of the 20th, when "general quarters" was sounded. One minute earlier, the *Trinity* had reported torpedo wakes "from aft to port". At 0537 *Edsall* picked up "an echo bearing 290 degrees…distance 2,300 yards." Having asked *Alden* if she wanted help and receiving a reply in the negative, *Edsall* : "manoeuvred to rejoin *Trinity* and screen between submarine and convoy". That was the extent of *Edsall*'s action at this time, apart from various changes in her patrolling station to protect the *Trinity* on the rest of the journey into Darwin.

Later the same day, at 1645, *Edsall* put once more to sea in company with *Alden*. At 1859 that evening the three Australian corvettes were sighted, busily searching for their submarine contact and hurling depth charge after depth charge into the sea. Signals between the corvettes and the American destroyers soon established the situation. Half an hour later, at 1929, on the edge of the oil slick already generated from depth charging, an underwater contact was gained, and *Edsall* exchanged her information with a nearby corvette, noting that "He evidently had contact also".

At 1940 – twenty to eight – after various contacts gained and courses changed, *Edsall* launched her first depth charges. A pattern of five was fired; however only three explosions were noted.

Nothing significant happened, *Edsall* again "keying into slick either side of target", presumably meaning she was aiming sonar signals into these areas. This was the full extent of *Edsall*'s part in the action.

USS ALDEN

The executive officer of *USS Alden*, Lieutenant EE Evans, submitted a brief report stating the ship's role in the sinking of the submarine. Providing part of an anti-submarine screen for the incoming convoy, *Alden* was a "flush deck" elderly destroyer of 1190 tons. Built in 1919, she was the same four funnel type as the ill-fated *USS Peary* – later to meet her end in Darwin Harbour – and was commanded at the time of the *I-123*'s attack by Lieutenant Commander LE Coley.

At 0540 on the 20th January *Alden* operated her sonar in response to a signal from *USS Trinity* to the effect that a torpedo wake had been sighted. Gaining a positive contact at a distance of 1200 yards, *Alden* dropped two depth charges at 0541, the detonation causing her to lose the sonar's signal. Sonar contact was not regained, despite patient searching: *Alden*'s commander later concluded in his report that the wakes of the ship's many tracks around the area made it impossible to obtain a further contact. Subsequently *Alden* broke off the search at 0700 to continue her role in providing the submarine screen for *USS Trinity*.

The following afternoon, *Alden*, like *Edsall*, put to sea to hunt the submarine that had attacked her convoy. However, the destroyer remained quite clear of the action area, only gaining a sonar contact at 1955 that evening, upon which she dropped depth charges. The following morning *Alden* gained another contact just before 0900, and fired depth charges once more.

It is worth noting as a postscript to the action, that while the credit for the sinking goes to *Deloraine* (and quite rightly so), the action may very well not have had the successful conclusion it did without the aircraft involved, and to a limited extent the other corvettes concerned, at least if the depth charge detonation near *I-124*'s conning tower was not the *coup de grace*. It must be remembered that the hunted submarine could

Some of Deloraine's crew on deck immediately after securing from action stations. A film of oil covers the water to the ship's starboard side, either produced by the depth charges or a successful strike. (Stan Hale)

hear her pursuers, and may have sighted them more than once. If the action had been a simple one of single submarine versus single corvette, the action might have turned out differently. Just as *Deloraine*'s avoidance of the torpedo and immediate attack was a testimony to an efficient team, so too was the overall action a tribute to ships, aircraft and their crews working together. And the success of *Deloraine* is a reflection on the high probability that any other corvette concerned would have acquitted herself as honourably.

It is interesting in the light of these descriptions to analyse some of the various descriptions of the action that have been written since. As mentioned before, many accounts seem to credit a mix of American and Australian ships – perhaps a sop to the alliance? WJ Holmes' *Undersea Victory* is the most generous: the end of *I-124* is awarded to the American destroyer and all three Australian ships. Arnold Lott's *Most Dangerous Sea* accredits the sinking to: "*Edsall* and some Australian minesweepers". However, it is notable that these, and Roscoe's cited above, are American publications. That *Alden* did make a brief attack on a submarine on 19 January, 1942 is undeniable, but having asserted her presence she was then bound to continue her escort duty – the *USS Trinity* was a valuable asset that could hardly be left unprotected. *Edsall* had no part in this first attack. Later that day *Edsall* did launch depth charges against a possible submarine – but some six hours after *Deloraine*'s decisive action. An examination of the timing of the various attacks shows clearly that *Edsall* did not contribute to the sinking of the Japanese submarine.

(Endnotes)

1   See p. 85. Gill's history sources the credit from *German, Italian and Japanese U-Boat Casualties* during the war. (Comd 6843, June 1946) p. 31.

2   USN Naval Historical Center. Dictionary of American Naval Fighting Ships, http://www.history.navy.mil/danfs/e2/edsall-i. htm, accessed 18/10/10.
     Winslow, WG. *The Fleet the Gods Forgot, The U.S. Asiatic Fleet in World War II*. Naval Institute Press, Annapolis, USA 1982. (p.40)

3   *USS Langley*: seaplane tender, was built in 1912 as the collier *Jupiter*, converted to an aircraft carrier in 1920, and modified further to become a seaplane tender in 1937. 10, 050 tons, four 5-in. guns, 15 knots. Later heavily damaged by Japanese bombers south of Java, 27 Feb 1942, and subsequently sunk by a US destroyer – details courtesy Gill and Department of Naval History, US Navy.

HMAS Lithgow loaded with troops later in the war. Note the disruptive camouflage scheme.
(Royal Australian Navy)

USS Edsall in the 1920s. By 1942 she was outdated but still serving. Her four funnels are a distinctive feature; like the rest of her class she was known as a "four-stacker". An identical-looking ship of the same class – USS Peary – was to go down fighting in Darwin Harbour a month after the I-124 action. (US Naval Historical Centre)

Deloraine crewmembers in a relaxed moment, January 1942: (l/r) Leading Stoker Aub Lindley; Stoker Frank Marsh; (seated) Leading Signalman Douglas Fraser. (Frank Marsh)

Lieutenant Commander Kouichi Kishigami (Atsuko Kishigami)

CHAPTER 7

– DEATH ON THE SEABED

The first attempt to make contact with the now crippled *I-124* was made by the corvette *HMAS Katoomba* during the evening of 20 January. After *Deloraine* had rejoined the area upon acquiring more depth charges from *Vigilant*, *Katoomba* made an attempt to drag for the submarine, according to her log, using a grapnel: "hoping to bring up his aerial or something tangible". Soon the weighted hook made contact with the submarine below, but when pressure was applied the grapnel broke free, and when recovered, it was found that "two prongs were almost straightened out". Colin Price, then the Petty Officer in charge of engines, remembers seeing: "...the tines were torn and jagged indicating to me that the *I-124* had boom-net or mine cable cutting lines fitted fore and aft". *Katoomba* then stayed over the spot for the night, and in the morning, to: "be sure he would remain there for all time" dropped four more depth charges.

Later that morning diving was attempted from the boom defence vessel *Kookaburra*. The local boom vessels, a 135 foot design modeled on the British Net class, were sturdy, hard-working little ships, with a pair of vast horns at the bow, used for manoeuvring the booms and floats attached to anti-submarine nets. Armed with a single aft-mounted three-inch gun, and machineguns, they had a top speed of 9.5 knots and were rarely used outside harbours. For *Kookaburra*'s crew of 32, commanded by Lieutenant Harold Gaskill RANVR, it must have been an unlikely outing. From the largely protected work manning the boom, they were now moored right in the middle of a combat zone.

At 0415, early in the morning of 21 January, the Australian ship left harbour, and at 1110 her deck log reports: "Arrived at scene of operations". Soon *Kookaburra* was "anchored fore and aft in position", and at 1627 a diver descended. After a six minute dive another diver was sent down; he made a 15 minute descent and upon his return the boom vessel returned to harbour. The same process was carried out the following day, with one dive made, and again on the 23rd. Then followed a break of some days until the 26th of January, when *Kookaburra* left harbour at 0100 in the morning. Her deck log is short on detail, noting merely that at 0745 she: "Arrived at scene of operations" and weighed anchor after a long day at 1820, but returned to the scene of operations at 0050 the following morning. *Kookaburra* then left for home again at 0740.

The Navy divers – their identity is not known[a] – were clearly not making headway; perhaps for a number of reasons: inexperience, equipment quality and the strong tides of that period of the month all perhaps being contributing factors. A signal on the 23rd reports: "Diving has been unsuccessful owing to tide. Dark shape has been seen but not reached by diver." The diary of a Leading Telegraphist – JA Rogers – who was on board *Lithgow*, suggests "Diver down but only for 1 mins due to tide rip. Located Sub. No 1, which is a large one, probably I class. Could be minelayer. " Diving was abandoned, with one signal noting that neap tides began on the 26th.

Given this frustration the RAN turned for help to its American allies. In Darwin at the time of *I-124*'s sinking was *USS Holland*, a submarine repair vessel. The US Navy agreed to help, but with a proviso about *Holland*'s deployment. Although the big ship – 483 feet long and displacing 8,199 tons – was fully equipped for descents onto such a wreck, a diving party was embarked on the boom vessel *HMAS Kookaburra*, as this was not nearly so significant a target to place into a combat area where submarines were active.

Holland, a valuable target in time of conflict, was enjoying an extended stay alongside in Darwin, where ship duties in these early days of the war were largely interrupted only by shore patrols and a little rest and relaxation, although the crew was finding Darwin restrained by contrast with later ports their ship would visit. *Holland*'s war diary remarks:

> Darwin was noteworthy from a medical point of view for two reasons: first, a slight outbreak of dengue fever occurred that affected about ten percent of the personnel; and second, it was the only port in which no venereal diseases were acquired. This was in sharp contrast to the next port, Tilatjap, Java, where during eleven days in port in February, 1942, sixteen cases of gonorrhoea were admitted to the sicklist.

The sojourn of some of the crew was to be interrupted for the last days of January. In response to the confirmed submarine sinking outside the harbour, a team of 16 divers and attendants was assembled, and transferred to the *Kookaburra*.

The divers who had made the previous attempts from the Australian ship were able to ensure the submarine was quickly re-found. Homer White, a crewman from the *Holland*, remembers that "Divers from *H.M.A.S. Kookaburra*, from memory, I could be wrong, guided our launch to the *I-124*." Whether the Australian divers made further descents is unclear, but this may have been so: Colin Price from *Katoomba* remembers talking to one of them:

> During the period when *Katoomba* was being repaired I spoke to a diver from

---

a   *Katoomba's* PO Colin Price remembers speaking to a diver based on *Platypus* who said he had walked the length of the submarine. It may have been the case, to form an Australian team, the local NOIC rounded up all nearby qualified RAN divers for the attempt.

Platypus. He told me that he had walked along the deck of the *I-124* and found the hatches had been sprung but made no mention of having entered the vessel. Perhaps the *Plats* carried divers. He did say that there were mines still in the racks and I think he mentioned 16.

The diving party from *USS Holland* arrived on *Kookaburra* at the buoyed location of the submarine on 26 January. Two reports of the subsequent diving operations are in existence, both from Captain JW Gregory USN, the commanding officer of *USS Holland*. The first is addressed to the Naval Officer in Command (NOIC), Darwin, and the second to the Commander in Chief, Asiatic Fleet. The reports were largely similar, and contain information from the commanding officer of diving operations, Lieutenant Commander RE Hawes.

The first report describes the initial search for the submarine as unsuccessful: the first and second divers not finding the wreck at all in the brief "no-decompression" time of 16 minutes – all they were allowed on the bottom. The third diver, however, located "... a large gully about 15 feet across 4 to 6 feet deep, which is believed to be where the submarine first hit bottom". After the *Kookaburra* was moved and a fourth diver sent down the wreck was positively identified: "...a large submarine. One hatch apparently blown open. Unable to make out any identification. Also located 2 other hatches but did not reach conning tower."

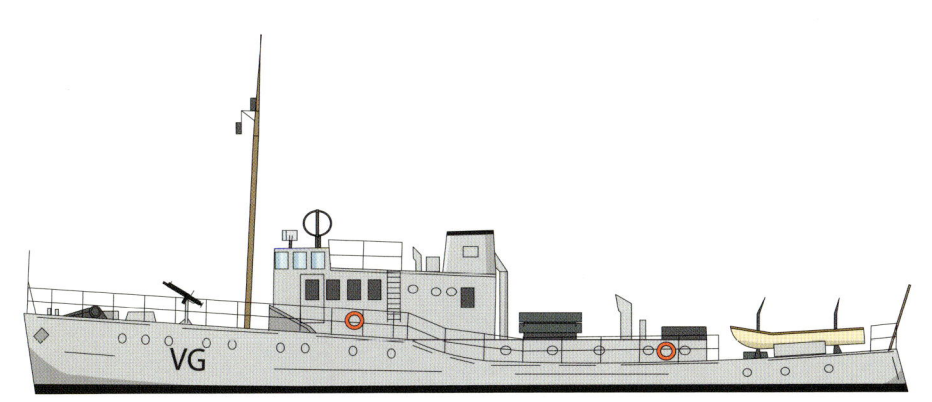

HMAS VIGILANT

Type: patrol boat   **Built:** *1938*   *Displacement: 106t*   **Length:** *102ft*   **Beam:** *16.4ft;*
Speed: *13½ kts*   **Armament:** *machine guns*

Vigilant was a civilian patrol vessel, requisitioned for naval service in 1940. On 20 January 1942 she was loaded with depth charges and then replenished HMAS Deloraine at sea. This was an example of the many duties carried out by the small fleet of naval small ships in Darwin.

Graphic by Peter Ingman

HMAS Katoomba lying at anchor. She dragged for I-124 after the submarine had been crippled by HMAS Deloraine. (Royal Australian Navy)

HMAS *KATOOMBA*

Katoomba, another *Bathurst* class corvette, had a back-seat role in the attack on *I-124*. On 21 January, the day after *Deloraine*'s attack, the corvette was under the command of Commander AP Cousin, RANR(S). Operating in the area of the previous attack, at 0800 *Katoomba* launched four depth charges on top of a submarine contact. At this stage divers on board *Kookaburra* were proceeding to the spot where it was presumed a submarine was sunk. As *Kookaburra* came into sight *Katoomba* received a signal from *Lithgow* to the effect that a submarine had been sighted off Cape Fourcroy, Bathurst Island – about 60 miles northwest of Port Darwin and a likely spot for submarines to intercept shipping traffic. Joining up with *Deloraine* the *Katoomba* steamed off towards the north and soon sighted *USS Edsall*, also making her way to the new contact.

Arriving in the area after an hour's steaming *Katoomba*, *Deloraine* and *Edsall* sighted *Lithgow*, patiently maintaining a faint contact with what was thought to be a submarine. A Catalina aircraft[b] had joined the search, and soon signaled a contact to the ships, sending the message: "I will circle sub". The two Australian ships turned back on their original course and now steamed towards the south-east. *Lithgow* signaled she had seen oil rising, and *Katoomba*'s Commander Cousin surmised: "I then presumed Submarine had started to surface but on seeing "Catalina" had dived and struck the bottom heavily opening up some oil tanks."

---

b   Suggestions of a Dutch Dornier tri-motor aircraft have been made; however this has been discounted by Dutch records.

At 0930 the Catalina was "circling steadily" and *Katoomba* also sighted oil. At 0948 four depth charges were launched, the resulting explosion being so great *Katoomba* had wiring damaged on board. Oil was seen rising after the depth charge explosion. While *Katoomba* attended to repairs *Deloraine* continued the attack, and at 1130 *Katoomba* was ready with her second set of charges – this time with the settings increased to 250 feet.

Over the next two days *Katoomba* carried out other depth charge attacks, and unfortunately in the early hours of the 23rd was involved in a collision with the *USS Pecos*, an oil tanker. Petty Officer Colin Price, asleep below, remembers being awakened: "by an awful crash, grabbing my life belt…I rushed up on deck". The ship had sustained heavy damage and was subsequently taken in tow by *Lithgow*.

On the following morning of the 21st, at 0749, *Edsall* engaged an underwater contact. This time she dropped six depth charges, with five exploding. At 0802 one charge was dropped, due to problems with the depth charge throwers. After being joined by "two corvettes and one plane" the search was broken off, only to be rejoined at 0948. *Edsall*, reporting that the other ships had the situation "well in hand" decided to keep clear while runs onto the target were made. After examination of the oil slicks *Edsall's* report suggests "Seems to be two subs down in this area about 3/4 mile apart." A sighting of *USS Alden* was made: she reported being low in depth charges, and *Edsall*, with a good supply, decided to stay "to hunt this cripple." In company with the aircraft, *Edsall* continued the search, but when no further contacts was made and a rain squall worsened conditions, returned to port at 1315.

The fifth diver's report was comprehensive, and reflects a special interest in the hatches fitted to the submarine:

> …reported gaskets blown out of two other hatches abaft conning tower; a built in hatch at conning tower with hatch at top, a V shaped well at forward part and abreast conning tower about 15 to 20 foot long and 6 feet inside. Apparently peace time boat stowage. A small door open on conning tower with valve wheels exposed, believed to be salvage air manifold. Antenna ran from stern to conning tower….Did not locate gun, says he was about 15 steps forward of conning tower. Hatch blown open had dogs bent but no wheel inside for locking as we have. At each hatch there were two pad eyes also an air connection. The blown out gasket was cut from the after hatch. The hatch blown open was nearest conning tower. Gasket on second hatch was bulging out. Colour of submarine black but

was covered with slight coating of light colored mud. Ship was on an even keel. No bubbles visible. No damage of any kind noted to hull or decking other than condition of hatches.

This diver appears to have made a very accurate examination, as according to her construction drawings *I-124* indeed has a well for boat stowage aft of the conning tower. Further, while the drawings show the deck gun to be fairly close to the conning tower forward, actual pictures of *I-124* have the gun closer to the midway point between the conning tower and the bow. A sixth diver was sent down, and he verified the report of the previous visit. Then with the divers' air supply exhausted the *Kookaburra* returned to Darwin, arriving in the early hours of the morning.

THE MISSING GUN

In these dive reports made immediately after the sinking the absence of a gun forward of the conning tower is of interest. This is puzzling, and indeed may have given rise to a number of later reports of dives on the wreck; reports which suggested no gun, an aircraft hangar instead, and various other differences. The diversity of these reports have of course led to speculation that a second submarine was sunk in the vicinity.

This mine-laying submarine series carried a gun mounted forward of the conning tower, and with the then current philosophies of submarine operations it is unlikely she would have had it removed. It was quite in order during World War II for submarines to surface to attack previously torpedoed targets with their surface gun in order to finish them off. Despite their recent entrance to the sea war the Imperial Japanese Navy was fully conversant with surface combat procedures, as they were used extensively by the German Kreigsmarine in the Battle of the Atlantic, and indeed had been common submarine combat technique since World War I.

In later years dives which were carried out on the wreck of *I-124* did confirm the presence of the foredeck gun. Why then was the gun not reported during the *Holland* divers' explorations? The answer to this question is understood perhaps more by an experienced diver than a land person....

At around 40 metres on scuba or surface air the limits of air diving are being reached, at least for many divers. Even experienced divers operating at this depth can begin to suffer from nitrogen narcosis, sometimes known as "rapture of the deeps". Due to the poisoning with nitrogen of the diver's blood supply to the brain, a variety of alarming effects can be experienced. These range through a variety of symptoms. One is an inability to perform simple tasks involving logical

HMAS Kookaburra before her departure for Darwin. (Royal Australian Navy)

thought, such as adding up numbers on an underwater writing pad – the inscribed numerals, apart from being simply the wrong ones, resemble the handwriting of a drunk. Other divers may experience hallucinations or outright panic: a diver known to the author on a deep dive with his wife was suddenly "rescued" by his partner, who was under the impression the air in his tank was poisoned, and she was quite determined to save him from this by turning his air off. The cure for nitrogen narcosis is simple – ascend. Divers who have to work often past these depths and beyond breathe a "mixed gas", but this is not readily available – and was certainly not available to the *Holland* divers, who were probably using a DESCO helmet set and surface air.[c]

So perhaps "fifteen steps forward of the conning tower" was in fact five, or perhaps behind the conning tower? Perhaps, but nitrogen narcosis has less of an impact on experienced divers. However, the dive conditions on the *I-124* site should not be underestimated. The *Holland's* team was diving in the Wet season, at all hours, and visibility may have been extremely limited - perhaps only a metre or so. "Fifteen steps" is also a measure of the diver's boot; a distance of two metres or less. Perhaps this with poor visibility meant the gun was not seen further along

c   The author, whose diving is confined to SCUBA, is indebted to Mr Neil Molloy for his advice on helmet diving. DESCO stands for Diving Equipment and Salvage Company; the helmet used in January 1942 was probably succeeded by the USN Mark 5, perhaps one of the most famous helmets used. The helmet had air pumped to it from surface lines, considerably limiting the diver's mobility.

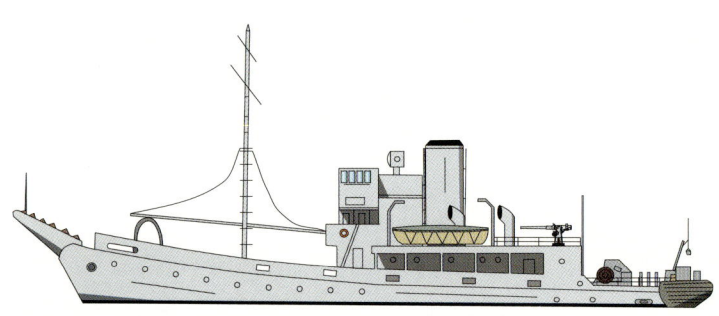

HMAS KOOKABURRA

Type: Modified Net Class Boom Defence Vessel

Builder: Cockatoo Docks & Engineering Company, Sydney, NSW

Commissioned: 28 February 1939   *Displacement:* 533 tons

Length: 135 feet   *Beam:* 26'6 feet

Armament: 1 x 3 inch HA/LA gun;   2 x .303 inch Maxim MG

Machinery: Triple expansion, single screw, 450 hp

Speed: 9.5 knots   *Complement:* 32

HMAS Kookaburra was the first specialised RAN Boom Defence Vessel. Commissioned in early 1939, she was used for training at Sydney and duties in Darwin before proceeding to the latter base permanently in 1940. Here she helped maintain and patrol the long Darwin anti-submarine boom net. She proved too small for some of the roles, and her stern would raise above the sea when reeling in the heaviest parts of the boom. For this reason, the subsequent Boom Defence Vessels were significantly larger and contained additional stern ballast. Nevertheless, she was a useful vessel and after the sinking of I-124, it was divers from Kookaburra that first tried to locate the wrecked submarine.

Graphic by Peter Ingman

the casing. There are many reasons why the gun was not seen. In summary, the *Holland*'s divers missed the gun, but they were on the right submarine.

Later dives have indeed confirmed the presence of the foredeck gun. Sub-Sea Services, a professional diving company, diving in 1973 in one of the many aborted attempts at salvage, reported the weapon in accurate detail. Furthermore, in 1985, writing to the Secretary of Federal Department of The Arts, Heritage and the Environment, Captain Partington, the Director of Naval Operations, reported divers from *HMAS Curlew*, who were inspecting the wreck because of reports of loose mines, had confirmed the presence of the gun. "...the 5.5 inch gun which is in good condition with the barrel trained level fore and aft."

TRAPPED INSIDE?

There have been a host of reports written about the end of *I-124* over the last fifty years. Many of these reports claim that American divers standing on the hull heard the Japanese crew, trapped inside, tapping on the hull. The story is a persistent one, occurring in most press articles about *I-124*, and still persisting in modern times, as seen in David Hancock's article "Jap Subs are still menacing Darwin" in *The Australian* (April 1989), which suggests "loud tapping" was heard from inside. An interesting feature is that most reports mention that the divers who heard the noises were from the American ship *Black Hawk*, not the *Holland*, which had indeed sent divers down to investigate.

One of the first occurrences of this story was contained in an article in a 1973 edition of *The Sun* newspaper. There too the suggestion was made that *Black Hawk* was involved. The article centred around the recent discovery of the submarine and highlighted salvage diver Harry Baxter's role. Detailing the aftermath of the sinking, writer Gavin Souter reported:

> Later in the day, a diver from the fleet repair ship *USS Black Hawk* went down 167 feet to the dying *I-124*. He walked the full length of her deck, and heard the sound of tapping from inside. It was no good tapping in 1942. The corvettes and the repair ship sailed away, and in due course the crew of the *I-124* died.

US Navy diver Elmer Feltz makes ready for a descent in "standard dress". (Elmer Feltz)

The "tapping story" was repeated in Vaughan Mawbey's article "The $2 million Graveyard!" in *Australasian Post*, March 1981; but without specific reference to a ship name. In Denis Williams' *Sunday Press* article "The Sub with a Million Secrets" of April 1984, the aftermath of the sinking is described in similar terms: "Later in the day, a diver from the *USS Black Hawk* went down and walked the length of the sub's hull. He heard the sound of tapping. Trapped Japanese were signaling they were still alive."

Iris Nesdale, in her examination of the role of small ships in World War II - *The Corvettes*, states:

> ...on the following day a diver from the US Fleet Repair ship, Black Hawk, went
> down and walked the length of the Japanese raider. It was said that tapping sounds
> from inside the submarine could be heard, but in the 1940s rescue equipment was
> not yet available, and nothing could be done to help. [p. 26]

Nesdale's report contains the same ship name that many other reports of "tapping" include – that of *USS Black Hawk*. However, *Black Hawk*'s log does not contain any accounts of dives made at the time.

It is indeed probable that sections of the sunken submarine remained sealed. By means of watertight doors and a well-trained crew, any submarine commander could hope to overcome flooded compartments, and indeed the means of repairing the damage, pumping out the water and getting the boat moving again were well understood and practised in World War II. Given the ferocity and weight of the attack against her however, it is almost certainly the case that *I-124* was damaged enough so that she was fatally crippled, perhaps in the stern sections so that power to move had gone. Only a close examination of the wreck can reveal exactly how damaged she was. But it is unlikely that every compartment was flooded, and although some of the crew may have been killed in the initial attack, there is every reason to presume that some survived.

Escape from a sunken submarine is certainly possible, and while it can be life-threatening, the manoeuvre can be made even without escape equipment. Certainly there are well-documented stories of submariners escaping from sunken boats by opening a hatch after equalising the inside and outside pressures and then ascending in a bubble of air. Escape from *I-124* at this depth would certainly have been possible, but according to later dive reports, it seems that the severity of the depth charging was such that any possible escape routes were sealed. An escape chamber on a submarine must be an air-lock that can be flooded in a controlled manner – any opening of say, the main hatches in the conning tower would certainly have been virtually impossible due to the pressure of water outside on the hatch.

EARLY ESCAPES FROM SUNKEN SUBMARINES

The inventor Wilhelm Bauer, a corporal in the Bavarian Light Horse Artillery, launched an undersea boat called the *Brandtaucher* at Kiel in 1849. Some time later, Bauer and his crew of two ended up sixty feet deep with the nose of their craft buried in the mud and the stern of it nearly stove in. Bauer finally talked his two companions into flooding the craft so inner pressure would equal exterior pressure, thus allowing them to escape. Each man went up in his individual air bubble like, Bauer said, a champagne cork. They all survived without injury to earn a place in history as the first free escape from a submarine without an escape lung or similar device.

Chief Petty Officer Brown escaped from the collision and sinking of HM submarines *E-4* and *E-41* in the Irish Sea in July of 1915 in much the same way. As the only remaining crewmember in the engine room, he flooded the engineroom, opened a hatch and ascended in a rush of air to the surface 60 feet away. He survived. (Courtesy John. D. Anthony)

Escaping submariners have also used the Stanke Hood, an inflatable life vest with a zippered hood covering the head. The idea of a formal escape hatch is described by Stan Crapo, who advises that: "the easiest way to exit a submerged submarine in an emergency was via an escape trunk. A hatch to sea above, a hatch to the interior of the boat below; space for a couple of men in between. You enter, close and seal the lower hatch, admit air from the boat's air flasks until the pressure inside the trunk is that of the sea, open valves to flood the trunk with sea water and vent air, open the upper hatch, and go for the surface. Linkages and valving inside the submarine near the escape trunk allow closing the upper hatch and draining water from the trunk so it may be used over and over to permit the escape of many crew members".

What would have been the eventual fate of any trapped crewmembers? Certainly not a pleasant one. The submarine's interior air would already have been fouled by hours of confinement, and added to that would be the chlorine gases emitted from the boat's batteries and diesel fumes from the fuel on board. Death from lack of air was hours away at most, but perhaps the surviving members of the crew took the way out that was common to Japanese warriors: *seppuku*, or *harakiri*, as it was usually known, the ritual disembowelment of oneself.[d]

---

d   But not necessarily by this method. The crew of *Midget No. 21*, one of the submarines that attacked Sydney harbour and sunk *HMAS Kuttabul* on 1 June 1942, killed themselves when their submarine was depth charged and sent to the bottom of the harbour. An examination of the bodies of Lieutenant Keiu Matsuo and Petty Officer Masao Tsuzuku found they had died as a result of self-inflicted revolver shots. Some hours previously the crew of *Midget No. 14* - Lieutenant Kenshi Chuma and Petty Officer Takeshi Ohmori - had killed themselves by firing demolition charges when their submarine was caught in the harbour's anti-submarine net. (See Gill)

US Navy diver about to enter the water on a "diver's stage". (Elmer Feltz)

Did the *Holland* dive team hear knocking? Their arrival on the casing would certainly have been noticed by anyone inside: the divers were wearing "standard dress" diving rig, very different from the lightly equipped scuba diver setup seen around the world today. In 1942, Jacques Cousteau's scuba invention was still being perfected. The American divers were wearing a suit that resembled overalls which prevented the entry of water, a heavy copper helmet that was connected to the surface by an air-carrying line, and importantly in this context, cumbersome boots weighted with lead. The latter items would certainly have resounded on the hull as the divers walked its length.

However, Elmer Feltz, a dive attendant on the *Holland* dives and later a Chief Master Diver, is most emphatic about the team not hearing anything:

> In all my years of diving, and all of the dives I made on submarines, I don't believe there is any truth in the story that divers from the *USS Black Hawk* heard knockings from within any submarine. As I recall, there were only a few divers on the *USS Black Hawk*.

The story of men trapped inside may have had its genesis in the claims of a *Deloraine* crewmember, or at least a man who was loosely associated with the corvette. Mr Bob Laffer, a surveyor from Western Australia and an enthusiastic devotee of maritime history, recalls meeting a Bob Williams, who claimed to have been serving in *Deloraine* during the *I-124* engagement. Williams recounted to Laffer how *Deloraine*'s commander sent a diver down:

> He then went on to tell me that *Deloraine*'s commander, name of Donovan I think, sent a diver down to make sure that *I-124* was not foxing. The diver confirmed that the sub was buggered, and could hear the Japs inside. Then he got his gear tangled up in the sub's superstructure, and had to cut himself free, after closing the exhaust valve on his old fashioned diving suit. He rose very smartly to the surface and was pulled on board *Deloraine*.

However, Williams died shortly afterwards, and Laffer was unable to gain any more details. There are several problems with this account, which is contained in a letter from Laffer to Mike McCarthy of the WA Maritime Museum. It implies that *Deloraine* had easy access to a

HMAS Kookaburra at work on the Darwin boom net. Very few of the giant floats remain today – one can be seen by visitors to Darwin in Doctor's Gully outside the tourist attraction Aquascene. (Royal Australian Navy)

diver and all of his complicated equipment of the 1940s; and seems to imply that the dive was made immediately - perhaps on the afternoon of the 19th or on the following day. However, there is nothing in *Deloraine*'s reports to support this, and even if a diver had been put aboard from another vessel, the descent would have been reported. (The dive account too is flawed: divers do not "rise smartly" to the surface; they proceed at a steady 60 feet per 60 seconds or more slowly, to avoid decompression problems, or a massive barotrauma - an injury caused by expanding air within the body - a burst lung, for example.)

Deloraine crew members who have been asked about this story are unanimous in their opinion that no diving took place. Douglas Fraser confirms that "*Deloraine* did not carry out diving exploits on the submarine" and also says "I cannot recall any crewmember named either 'Bob' or 'Charles' Williams..." Crew member Len Crabbe confirms: "To the best of my recollection no dive took place from *Deloraine*" and he also recalls the *Kookaburra* dive and that "*Deloraine* stood by during the dive..." The Gunnery Officer from *Deloraine* - Lieutenant W. Eric Thompson - points out that "...no diver was sent down by *HMAS Deloraine*. Had we had a diving suit on board it would have been on my 'slop chit'. I do not recall such an item....regarding Bob Williams. I do not think that this man was a member of *Deloraine*'s crew." Crewmember Arthur Waller says: "I never remember a person by the name of Williams ever being in *HMAS Deloraine*". The crewlists from 31 December 1941, which are held in the Australian Archives, do not list the name of Bob Williams either.

However, crew member Len Crabbe remembers a Charles Williams on board at one time, who was a telegraphist, and he also remembers a Bob Williams: "...who I knew, serving in *HMAS Platypus* in Darwin at that time, and he lived in East Fremantle after the war." It is conceivable that this Bob Williams was on board *Deloraine* for some reason temporarily, which would explain why he is not remembered as a crew member. But even if this is so, this does not account for the absence of any record of diving taking place from *Deloraine*.

The most probable explanation is confusion on the part of someone who was getting memories of long ago mixed up, *Deloraine* commander's name being given wrongly being the least of it. Len Crabbe again confirms the identity of Bob Williams, identifying his former war mate as someone with an interest in horseracing:

> After the war he lived in East Fremantle and was involved in harness racing...I am
> certain he was the Bob Williams referred to all the way along, but it really surprises
> me Bob would make such a statement....whatever he said was misunderstood and
> as you suggest grown since then.

It is perhaps worth pondering the situation inside *I-124* if crew members remained alive after the final depth-charging. Surrounded by explosives and possessing engineering skills, would any crew members who knew they were going to die spend their final hours constructing booby traps for any divers who eventually did enter the submarine? Perhaps a far-fetched possibility, but penetration of the hull, in any case, even around 70 years later, would be dangerous indeed.

The submarine tender USS Holland, seen here with submarines alongside in San Diego in 1930. As a floating base ship for submarines, Holland would have been better equipped for underwater salvage operations than the RAN. However, there was no question of risking the valuable ship outside the relative sanctuary of Darwin Harbour, as continued operations by the Asiatic Fleet submarines depended on her. So diving teams from Holland were deployed from HMAS Kookaburra at the I-124 wreck site. (USN)

USS Peary in a tranquil moment. Her sinking in Darwin accounted for the biggest loss of life in a single ship in the February 1942 initial raid: survivor Dallas Widick later accounted for 91 men lost. Peary remained lost for some years after her sinking, despite efforts to locate her wreck by the War Graves Commission. In 1956 she was located by HMAS Quadrant, which passed over the wreck with depth sounders operating; the ship was quite a distance from where she began to go down, and probably had dragged her half-raised anchor as she sank to arrive in her final location off Darwin's Esplanade in 30 metres of water. (United States Navy)

CHAPTER 8

– A SECOND SUBMARINE?

The possibility that the attack was made on two boats, not one, is suggested by the attack reports from the commanding officers of both *HMAS Katoomba* and *HMAS Deloraine*. These both indicate contact during the attack with a second submarine some 5, 000 feet from the first "kill", which itself was definitely confirmed by oil coming to the sea surface. Depth charging on the second contact produced oil too. *Deloraine* even attacked another asdic echo on the 21st and again confirmed oil rising to the surface. *USS Edsall* joined this attack and examined oil coming from the spot: the commander's report says: "... seems to be two subs down in this area about 3/4 mile apart". But after investigating the matter the Royal Australian Navy decided later that there was in reality one submarine, and the credit for the sinking was awarded to *Deloraine*, quite in accordance with the opinions of the other two corvette commanders involved in the action.

Confirmation that there were indeed two submarines in the hunt is provided by the Japanese sources cited previously. *I-124*'s end was even heard by one of her sister boats: her war diary contains the significant passage: "Jan. 20. Submarine *I-123* heard an explosion from the direction of Submarine *I-124*".

Prior mention of *I-124* being "in company" is suggested for some time before *I-124*'s end. As underwater noise can be heard at considerable distance, it is conceivable that one boat heard the end of the other. David Stevens estimates that the two submarines would have been unlikely to have traveled together "as this would have increased their vulnerability". He also has provided figures from US missions to Japan at the end of the war, in which it was found that bearings on noise were possible at 40, 000 metres, or 40 kilometres distance. He mentions too that the water conditions off Darwin had been found to have given better than usual sonar performance. Modern figures of hydrophone performance are comparable: hearing underwater noise up to 60-80,000 yards away is not uncommon. Altogether, while there is plenty of evidence for saying that the two submarines were not exactly traveling "in company", they were in adjacent patrol zones. Certainly *I-123* heard the end of her sister ship.

The February raids by Japanese forces on Darwin more than avenged I-124. Barossa shown on fire in the left of this photograph; Neptuna is sinking on the right. (Historical Repository, HMAS Coonawarra, Darwin)

Depending on how close *I-123* was to her companion, accompanying the noise of any final explosion would have been other ominous sounds: the blowing and flooding of ballast tanks that accompanied *I-124*'s part-surfacing and crash dives; repeated depth charge explosions; the impact of bombs from the aircraft circling overhead, and perhaps the sound of the submarine's final impact on the seabed. Perhaps there would have been further sounds too. Analysis of the attacks made on the crippled boat suggest that she was able to make some distance after her sinking.

So while a second submarine, *I-123*, was present in the wider vicinity, she was never depth charged directly and it would seem that multiple attacks were made on the already disabled *I-124* and/or false contacts. However, the suggestion that there were indeed two submarine sinkings outside Darwin has always been a controversial part of *I-124*'s story, even up until modern times. In 1942 the attack reports were given careful scrutiny by the RAN's Anti-Submarine School. On 16 February the School submitted a report to the Navy Office. There they summarised their opinion: that "only 2 submarines were present", and that "it is highly probable that a second was also sunk." The report discussed "Hydrophone Effect" and attacks on oil and debris, and suggested that the submarine first attacked was crippled and leaking, and "crept away to the North East" before her final dispatch. The report concluded that the credit for the sinking of the first submarine should be given to *Deloraine* and if a second boat kill was confirmed, that should be accredited to *Katoomba*.

It should be noted, in support of the RAN's suggestion above, that the later diving did find what is described both as a "gully" and a "furrow" behind the stationary wreck, presumed at the time to be where the rapidly descending submarine first hit bottom. However, at the time, how far astern did this furrow extend? Could it have been in fact quite lengthy, and have been in fact caused by the mortally wounded *I-124* trying unsuccessfully to gain buoyancy, instead merely dragging herself along the bottom of the seabed? Such movement would of course produced both sonar noise and bubbles, perhaps even rupturing oil tanks, and therefore inviting the attacks that continued throughout the day.

The Australian forces certainly anticipated further combat, and made plans to catch any other submarines on the surface that night. Signals setting up a possible attack with a Hudson aircraft as spotter were made to *Lithgow*, *Deloraine* and the sloop *HMAS Swan:*

The floating dock in Darwin Harbour which provided maintenance facilities for ships up to the size of a corvette (here a boom defence vessel is inside the dock). HMAS Katoomba entered the dock after being badly damaged during a collision with USS Pecos just days after I-124 was sunk. She was there during the 19 February air attack, and despite being a perfect target gave enough defensive fire to deter the attackers. (Historical Repository, HMAS Coonawarra, Darwin)

Zealandia on fire and sinking by the stern. A rescue boat can be seen on the water. (Ken Cossums)

Hospital ship Manunda on fire, with a rescue boat in the foreground. (Ken Cossums)

My (sic) 0536 25th January 1 Hudson will remain vicinity of submarine until dark. Submarine should therefore be at dark within 10 miles of reported position and will probably surface during the night.

However, a second victory was not to be. There is some evidence of other signals of submarine sightings over the next few days, and certainly there seems suggestion on the 23rd that *Edsall* sighted what was probably *I-123* on the surface and attacked, but nothing in the reports of the three remaining minelayers suggests they were targeted. One interesting report, contained in a post-war chronology of the conflict in the north suggests that a surfaced submarine was seen on the 20th by Lieutenant Andrew Smith RANVR, commanding the ex-mission lugger *HMAS St Francis*, although the brief mention does not specify when in the day the supposed submarine was seen.

Although speculation has continued up until the present day about the existence of a second submarine being in the vicinity of *I-124*, there does not seem to be sufficient evidence to warrant such a claim. German and Japanese vessels lost in the war have been fully accounted for, or if missing are such a distance away that they cannot be in the area: we can safely presume that vessels listed as missing in the Atlantic are not likely to be in Australian waters, for example.

As a postscript, it might also be worth noting at this point that the immense number of contacts and attacks made during the two days of the *I-124* action were not unusual for a war scenario. Indeed, as former anti-submarine naval officer and now naval historian David Stevens points out, in wartime it is the usual practice for understandably apprehensive crews to fire first at a contact and ask questions later, and Stevens cites the instances of the 1982 Falklands War, where various possible contacts ranging from whales to false sonar returns received British fire. In *I-124*'s case, it seems evident that while it was certainly the case that there were plenty of genuine targets, there were also many possibilities that came in for their share of understandable attention.

It should further be noted that depth charging in WWII produced as a side-product of the explosion a degree of oily scum that could be easily mistaken for oil leaking from a damaged submarine, and indeed often was mistaken as such by inexperienced crews. Of course, such "evidence" could only serve as justification for another attack, and so on.

One naval history[a] has noted that while prewar gunnery training with live ammunition was common, no practice was held with live depth charges. Consequently, early in the war, crews often mistook the great surface upheaval resulting from the explosion of a depth charge as sure evidence of a "kill".

---

a   Auphan, Rear Admiral Paul. *The French Navy in World War II*. United States Naval Institute: Annapolis USA, 1959. (p.31)

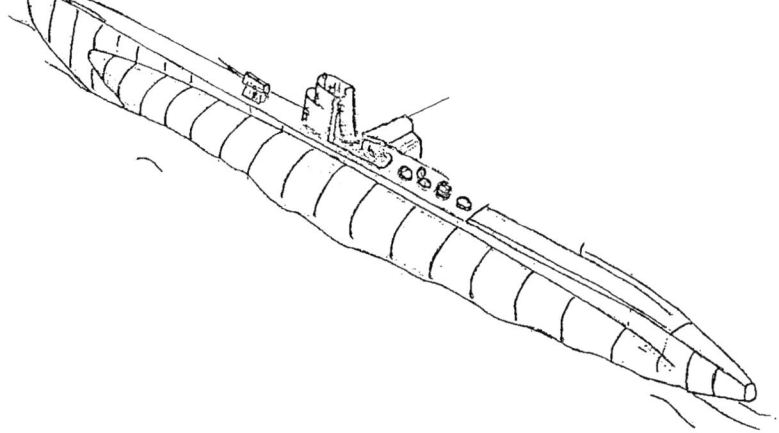

Chapter 9

– CODEBOOKS AND *HMAS SYDNEY?*

The story that *I-124*'s codebooks were recovered can be found in many articles and books. That *I-124* carried some sort of codebooks is not in doubt: all Japanese submarines were fitted with radio, and routine transmissions in wartime covered operations reports, orders, and logistical data. Like the stories of the Japanese crew being trapped inside the sunken submarine, stories of controversial cargo have also multiplied through the years, often growing in the telling.

One of the first books to mention the story is JD Potter's *Admiral of the Pacific*, written in 1965. Potter gives us an exciting but rather dubious story of the recovery, crediting Australian divers, rather than Americans, with codebook recovery:

> The *I-124* was sunk by depth charges in 150 ft of water off Darwin. Australian divers went down and found her nameplate. Then relays of other divers followed, armed with oxy-acetylene torches to cut open her hull. Patrol boats stood by while bubbles from the divers' breathing apparatus floated up to the surface. Soon objects from the sunken submarine, attached to lines by the divers, were being hauled to the surface. One of these was a thick black book heavily weighted with lead. It was a Japanese naval code book...[p. 124]

Norman Polmar and Dorr B. Carpenter's *Submarines of the Imperial Japanese Navy 1904-1945*, mentions the story:

> The *I-124*, with the division commander, Captain Keiyu Endo, embarked, sank with all those on board in water only forty feet deep. US Navy divers were sent down, entered the submarine, and removed naval code books, a godsend for the Navy codebreakers at Pearl Harbor. [p. 19]

The book, while a comprehensive survey of the Japanese submarine fleet's war, does not go into detail about the operations of each boat. *I-124*, while an interesting submarine from

A WWII US Navy dive team make ready for a descent. (United States Navy)

the point of view that she is still intact, did not have a lengthy war record, and therefore it is understandable that there are only such details as are briefly given above in many accounts.

Japanese sources also contain the story. Hiroyuki Agawa's book *Yamamoto Isoruleu Shinchusha*, which translated became *The Reluctant Admiral: Yamamoto and the Imperial Navy*, was published in 1969, and goes into some detail about the codebooks:

> ...in January that year contact had been lost with the submarine *I-124*, active in the Australian zone, with the duty of laying mines. The commands of both the Sixth (submarine) Fleet and Combined Fleet posted the submarine as missing after approximately one month, and ceased to worry further about the matter, but in fact the *I-124* had been encircled and sunk off Port Darwin, at dusk on January 20, by an American destroyer and three corvettes of the Australian navy. At the site of the sinking the sea was only forty feet deep, with clear water free from strong tidal currents, and the US navy immediately sent divers down from a submarine tender to cut open the *I-124*'s hull and bring up any important documents found inside. The documents thus recovered included a number of navy codebooks, among them the merchant vessel codebook. [(p. 307)]

There seem to be more than a few problems with this account. The vague location given, while correct, is wrong in being described as clear, 40 feet deep, and free of currents – the sinking site is exactly the opposite: deep for air diving at around 160 feet, with strong currents that give only a small window of diving twice a day. Secondly, visibility in these waters, while generally better than that inside the nearby harbour, is never really "clear" in the Wet season, where storms, rain and silt washed into the sea combine with the strong tides of the NT to reduce conditions. January, the month of the sinking, is the height of the Wet. Lastly, divers would hardly have cut through the hull of a submarine, a major task even on land, but rather have tried to gain access through hatches.

Whether the divers could have gained access through the hatches is an important point. It must be remembered that the *Holland* divers were wearing "standard dress" – a diving suit complete with heavy weighted boots and helmet. They were also breathing from a line connected to the surface, a considerably limiting factor. Homer White, a crewmember of the *Holland*, remembers talking to the divers when they returned from the *Kookaburra*, and they indeed commented that they couldn't have gained entrance through the hatches because of the small size of these openings. This was not reflected in an RAN signal of 28 January, which commented rather hopefully that "entry by divers is now being attempted". Perhaps on such small comments as this the stories began...

One of the most authoritative suggestions that *I-124* was indeed entered is found in Ed Drea's book *MacArthur's Ultra*, a comprehensive coverage of American radio interception and codebreaking. There it is reported that *I-124*'s codebooks were recovered and used against the Japanese:

> Shortly after the outbreak of the Pacific war, U.S. Navy divers had salvaged the Japanese navy's water transport "S" code books from a submarine that had been sunk off Darwin, Australia, in January 1942. With these documents in hand, navy cryptanalysts were able to read Japanese naval shipping messages and use the resulting intelligence to interdict some Japanese navy convoys. (p. 74)

In his notes, Drea gives as his source one Inagaki Takeshi, interviewed in editor Hasegawa Keitaro's book *Nihon Kindai to Senso, Vol. 1: Johosen no Haiboku (Japan's Modernity and War: Vol 1: Defeat in the Intelligence Wars)*, published in Tokyo in 1985. Takeshi stated that "Allied divers salvaged the Army Water Transport Code books". (p. 252) However, this claim was later refuted by two ex-members of the Central Bureau, the US codebreaking agency of the war – the codes were broken, they say, by expert analysis, not a lucky break gained from *I-124*'s codebooks.

Edward Drea confirmed in 1994 to this author his continuing opinion that the codebooks had been recovered: "To the best of my knowledge, Allied divers did enter the *I-124* and salvage Japanese naval code books". But how can this source be authenticated? Perhaps the best way is to find the original records of those recovery dives. However, the issue of secrecy is an obstacle here: there would be no point in carrying out an operation such as codebook recovery and

Stan Hale with an interesting cap tally in 1942. Cap tallies became simply "HMAS" once war broke out with Japan; Stan did not receive his for some time. (Stan Hale)

then allow that fact to be broadcast. The Japanese authorities, realising their code security had been compromised by the recovery of an entire set of books, would have changed their codes entirely. Therefore the dive operation records would have been given the very highest secrecy codes. No such records have been located.

Other accounts of the war in the Pacific, significantly, do not contain accounts of the Japanese codes being broken courtesy of *I-124*'s loss. *Silent Victory*, for example, written by Clay Blair Jr, does not mention the submarine, but instead devotes a substantial amount of the book to the efforts of the American codebreaking teams. Considerable success was gained by these people, Blair recounts, and he was in a position to know, having spent the war in American submarines and afterwards becoming a journalist who specialised in submarine stories. A supporter and admirer of Admiral Rickover, the "father" of the nuclear submarine fleet, Blair led a journalistic crusade to save Rickover from retirement, and was rewarded with many cruises and inspections of the nuclear fleet – in summary he knew a considerable amount about the submarine service and codebreaking combined. Instead of *I-124* being the lucky legacy of the codebreakers, Blair outlines in detail their real achievement: work on a succession of Japanese codes, which were often broken to a degree, with some of them being completely read. He accounts in detail for the codebreaking successes and failures that took place before Pearl Harbor, and details similar tides of fortune that took place throughout the war. But there is no magic sudden success that takes place in January or February 1942.

Perhaps the codebooks story came from somewhere else. There were indeed cases of codebooks being recovered from submarines in World War II. Blair gives an account of the sinking of the *I-7*, which was shelled off Kiska in 1943:

> ...the front half sank in very deep water, but the after half of *I-7* remained intact at 100 feet. Later, the navy sent the submarine rescue vessel *Florikan* to the scene. Seven divers entered the hulk and recovered "important documents" and "personal papers of value in intelligence work." (p. 418)

Another codebook recovery is described in WJ Holmes well-researched book *Double Edged Secrets*, which deals with the author's work on codebreaking during the war. Holmes mentions the story of the Japanese submarine *I-1*. This boat was attacked and sunk in 1943 by two New Zealand corvettes. Holmes describes (see page 124) how the crew escaped to shore, and subsequently buried some important codebooks. Meanwhile, American divers were recovering many codebooks and other valuable documents that had been left behind. Did accounts like these give substance to *I-124*'s story?

There certainly is a basis in fact for believing that an attempt to recover codebooks was planned. An annex to *Holland*'s reports, dated 6 February, 1942, was later attached. This brief letter is from JW Wilkes, the Commander Submarines, US Asiatic Fleet. He was writing at the time to his Commander in Chief. As we have seen previously, Wilkes devotes a paragraph to the codebooks:

> 4. It is possible that the sunken submarine holds documents which would be invaluable for future prosecution of the war. When circumstances become stabilized and permit it, it is requested that arrangements be made for attempting retrieving (sic) such documents. Lieutenant Commander R.E. Hawes is now assigned to the *Holland* and is available for organising a party for this purpose.

However, it is notable that the letter is classified as "Secret". Higher levels of security, such as "Most Secret", were available but were obviously not thought necessary – the reverse of the precautions that would have surrounded such an operation if the codebooks were essential and destined to be of high importance. The main paragraph of the letter is devoted instead to the quality of the hatch gaskets, as indeed are the bulk of *Holland*'s dive reports, once the initial description of the dives and submarine are concluded.

It is worth noting that as late as 1990 the codebook story was still making the newspapers. Max A. McDonald from the "International Naval Research Organisation" wrote to the *NT News* in

December of that year. He claimed that: "The wreck was visited by US divers the following day. All confidential papers, and a complete set of coded books which allowed the Americans to read Japanese naval signals, invaluable towards victory at Midway, were removed from the wreck."

Other authoritative accounts of the naval war do not give *I-124*'s codebook recovery as a reason for Japanese defeat. Masanori Ito's *The End of the Imperial Japanese Navy* does not mention any codebooks being intercepted, but rather says instead that success in the Battle of Midway was due to:

> ...brilliant intelligence work and the amazing success of American experts in breaking Japanese communications codes. It was the same remarkable success that six months earlier had given indication that Japan was about to go to war... blame must be placed on Japan's relaxed security measures. This relaxation of security was attributable directly to the fantastic victories Japan had enjoyed early in the war. [(p. 61)]

Hashimoto similarly offers no excuses:

> The Battle of Midway took place on June 4, 1942. The Japanese Navy, excelling in carrier strength and flushed with victory after the Hawaiian attack, was unaware that operational secrets had leaked out. And so we fell into the trap laid by the enemy, who was forewarned of our movements. [(P.49)]

That the divers from *USS Holland* did not enter the submarine is on record. Chief Bosun Ralph Snyder, one of the divers, placed on record in 1990 his statement concerning the matter, in a signed, witnessed statement:

> I was assigned in the task force that dived on a sunken Jap submarine for about 2 days. She was down in about 200 ft of water...I recall two dives made on the sunken ship...The depth of the dive required 1st Class Diver. I recall nothing but the underwater inspection. We did not perform any salvage operations at that time....We did not enter the sunken ship because we would have sent two divers down at the same time – one to tend the other and the ship's entrance hatch. One problem was sharks attacking when the stage[a] hit the water. We used rifles to protect the divers. We did not have two divers down at once.

---

a   The diving "stage", *Holland* Chief Master Diver Elmer Feltz informs, "was a platform, that was lowered into the water. It was used for the diver to rest on while he was being brought up out of the water, during decompression".

Instruction on the 0.303 machinegun in a quiet moment onboard HMAS Deloraine. (l/r) Eric Thompson, Bill Hornery, G McAndrew, George Price. (Eric Thompson)

The end result of this first set of dives being surveys only coupled with the February attack on Darwin was that *I-124* was left unentered, with her secrets, if any, untouched. A thorough search of Navy records in America, carried out in 1989 by Commodore David Campbell (later Rear-Admiral), when he was the RAN's Naval Attache in Washington, did not yield any material suggesting entry either. And there are other reasons why the codebooks were not recovered.

Mike McCarthy of the Western Australian Museum argues convincingly that the divers would never have been able to penetrate the submarine sufficiently due to the bulky nature of their dress. It is certainly a good point, and when one remembers that these divers were trailing air lines which would have to be carefully pulled through hatches and narrow passages, possibly with torn metal everywhere, the argument against diver penetration seems logical. Lifting the submarine seems much more feasible. Louis Wiegand, a baker on board *USS Holland*, confirms that rumours on board ship immediately after diving concerned the piece of rubber gasket recovered, and also that entry into the submarine had not been effected, due both to the bulk of the divers' equipment and the small size of the entry hatches.

Barbara Winter in *The Intrigue Master*, proves that perhaps those codebooks were not as important as might be thought – and not worth the expensive and hazardous process of recovery. Her exhaustive analysis of Australian naval intelligence in WWII shows that:

> ...by the time a dive could have been made, the codes and ciphers that *I-124* might have carried were being read fairly well. By late December, some messages were read with a delay of nine to twenty hours....It was being read so well by February that the number of killed and wounded on Japanese ships was known. [129]

USS Langley was significant as the USN's very first aircraft carrier. But during the late 1930s the forward half of her flight deck was removed and she began serving as a seaplane tender. (US Navy)

Moving beyond codebooks, there have also been suggestions that *I-124* contained evidence relating to the sinking of the light cruiser *HMAS Sydney* some three months earlier. The story of the *Sydney* is well known, and was for years, before the discovery of her shipwreck in 2008 at once ended one of the great mysteries and tragedies of WWII. The basic facts give an insight into the controversy: how could a powerful cruiser, commanded by an experienced captain, be sunk with all hands by the *Kormoran*, a disguised German armed raider? The battle took place on 19 November 1941, and debate began at once as to how the loss could have happened, while searches for the wreck proved fruitless.

The debate over *HMAS Sydney's* disappearance prompted several books. Possible connections with a submarine were raised almost immediately after the Australian cruiser's loss: London's *Daily Express* reported on 1 December 1941, that "it was a torpedo which sank the cruiser *Sydney*... whether the torpedo was fired by the Nazi vessel or by an attendant submarine is uncertain." There were interpretations of a link in sketches made by a survivor of the *Kormoran*, and to add to the debate a report in the *Northern Times* in 1941 that small footprints had been sighted on a deserted beach north of Carnarvon. In addition there were a host of "interpretations" from various sources pointing to supposed Japanese links. David Hancock's "The Secret of *I-124*" in *People* magazine of May 1989, repeated the arguments held for some years of a former RAAF airman, Mr Ed Ferrier of Darwin, and which he had publicised in various magazines and newspapers.

Mr Ferrier suggested that the "real" reason the Japanese were opposed to postwar exploratory dives onto the wreck as being that *I-124* was involved in the sinking of *HMAS Sydney*. In a letter of Mr Ferrier's published in the *NT News* of 17 March 1989, he referred to "persistent rumors that a Japanese submarine was involved in the destruction of the *Sydney*". He speculated that: "I am tempted to wonder whether the real reason for the Japanese concern over *I-124* is the fear that its log book could still be legible or that it could contain artifacts which might provide evidence as to what really happened to *HMAS Sydney*".

In another letter to the *NT News*, in 1990, Max McDonald, (who we have met before with his claim of *I 124* diver penetration) and who gave his post-nominal as "International Naval Research Organisation", also suggested that: "The submarine *I-124*, was generally believed to be involved in the sinking of the cruiser *Sydney*..."

One of the secondary instigators of the "*Sydney* and submarine" suggestion was Michael Montgomery, author of *Who Sank the Sydney?* published in 1981. Montgomery, the son of *Sydney*'s navigator, derived his idea primarily from the sketch made by a *Kormoran* survivor; the sketch, it is suggested, contains shorthand code that implies involvement by a Japanese submarine. The story has, since the publication of Montgomery's work, been repeated in a number of other books, such as Rusbridger and Nave's *Betrayal at Pearl Harbor*, which repeated the story, merely giving *Who Sank the Sydney?* as the source. Thus the myth of the Japanese submarine has slowly been accepted as factually based.

It is not the intention here to debate Montgomery's suggestion - that has already been done more than adequately by other writers. (Readers interested in the debate are referred to Barbara Winter's authoritative *HMAS Sydney Fact, Fantasy and Fraud*, Tom Frame's excellent *HMAS Sydney: Loss and Controversy*, published in 1993, and Wes Olson's superbly researched *Bitter Victory: the Death of HMAS Sydney*, released in 2001.) It is interesting however, to look briefly at any possible *I-124* involvement.

Firstly, while Montgomery does not name *I-124*, he does suggest that Japanese submarines were

HMAS Sydney at home in Sydney harbour shortly before she was lost in November 1941. (Royal Australian Navy)

HMAS Sydney - "A" turret, with its gun housing destroyed and with the foredeck rent back over its twin gun barrels. The recent finding of the wreck finally put an end to odd theories about her final fate. (The Finding Sydney Foundation)

active in Australian waters at this time: "...twenty-seven I Class units had set out either from Japan itself or from submarine bases in the much nearer Carolines and Marshalls..."[(p.188).] Later he argues that: "All records of Japanese submarine movements were among the casualties of the post-surrender bonfire..." [(p. 195)] However, as may be seen from sources such as *A History of the Imperial Japanese Navy Submarine*, the movements of each unit of the submarine fleet can be determined: there is no record of *I-124* being in southern waters at that time. Tom Frame has also gone to great detail to show the movements of all Japanese submarines at that time; his analysis is further proof that *I-124* was not involved in the *Sydney* battle, and he specifically names *I-124* as being "in Japanese ports in early November preparing for operations in the South China Sea." [(p. 172).] Indeed, aside from the mine-laying submarine squadron, most of Japan's large ocean going submarines were involved in supporting or screening the Pearl Harbor attack force and were preparing to sail for the Hawaiian Islands when Sydney was sunk.

Finally, mere logical deduction proves that *I-124* is not the key to the sinking of *HMAS Sydney*:

- the *Sydney* loss was three months before *I-124*'s sinking, during a time when Japan was not involved in fighting the Allies;

- the Axis powers had a remarkable lack of co-operation during the war, a fact pointed out by Winter;

- if a Japanese submarine was involved in the sinking of *Sydney* it would not have been *I-124*. As a Japanese submarine could hardly have been accidentally in Western Australian waters at the time, any such choice of boat to aid and abet the *Kormoran* would not have been an old, noisy and unstable mine-laying submarine;

- the Japanese would hardly have prejudiced their future entry into the war by embarking on the sinking of a mere light cruiser – it is notable that Pearl Harbor was not prejudiced by many similar opportunities beforehand. Thomas Paine, who until recently headed the comprehensive Submarine Warfare Library in California, put the matter forcefully when writing to Mike McCarthy of the Western Australian Maritime Museum in 1990, when McCarthy was investigating *I-124*:

> The worst possible date for a Japanese submarine to have initiated undersea hostilities was 19 November 1941. Next morning the First and Second Submarine Squadrons carrying five midget subs for the critical strike against Pearl Harbor sailed in great secrecy from Kure and Yokosuka. On the eve of launching their concentrated strike against the U.S. Battle Fleet, on which their war strategy depended, the Imperial Japanese Navy would have been insane to risk alerting their peaceful target by prematurely torpedoing an RAN light cruiser.

Winter and Frame's books also provide comprehensive detail on this matter:

- and as to the presence of evidence of the *Sydney* sinking being contained within *I-124*, Japanese submarines would hardly have gone to sea during the war with anything written down about such a conspiracy, even if such controversial knowledge was known throughout the fleet.

The suggestion that such reports are within the wreck of *I-124* unfortunately passed into that great mass of urban myth that is often the preferred belief of many people. In the same league can be found suggestions that items of immense value are on board *I-124*, stories of a second submarine nearby, the suggestion that the submarine has a valuable cargo of mercury – all of which will be dealt with in later chapters. (The author also noticed this type of story in researching *Wrecks in Darwin Waters*: the wreck of the *USS Peary* contained gold; a midget submarine is in Darwin Harbour; crowds of partygoers went to sea on the lost *Booya* and the *Darwin Princess* as they left the wharves during the beginning of Cyclone Tracy... While there is some basis for the suggestion in the first, and a big party was hosted on *Booya* that fateful day, it is only by meticulous research that we are able to find out the truth in these matters.) As many researchers have shown, and the second governmental inquiry into the loss of Sydney concurred, there is no basis for suggestion that a Japanese submarine, and that includes *I-124*, was involved in the tragic loss of *HMAS Sydney*.

CHAPTER 10

– THE SALVAGE ATTEMPT BEGINS

On the night of 27 January *Kookaburra* returned, but weather conditions were not good. When the weather did not improve she returned again to port, with a recommendation for salvage being made on the results so far:

> Further exploratory diving is required before a recommendation for salving can be given. The bottom is hard sand but the submarine may lie in a trough now filled with silt. Her main ballast tanks are evidently intact and could probably be blown through the salvage air lines. The damaged hatches can be repaired so that the flooded compartments can be blown.

特設潜水母艦に横付けして補給作業中の伊21潜―第二次大戦中の光景であろう。乗員の立っている後甲板の
下方に、三段二列の機雷棚で構成された機雷庫があり、ここと2本の敷設筒と合わせて八八式あるいは八八式
改一機雷が42個搭載されている。三段の機雷棚のうち中段が後尾にある2個の敷設筒に通じており、各敷設筒

I-121 alongside, showing the deck section aft of the conning tower in some detail. This was described in great accuracy by a USN diving report dated 1 February 1942, with the basic details noted labelled above. (Maritime History Department, Japanese Self-Defence Agency)

An Australian signal sent on the 30th from NOIC Darwin suggests some discussion about salvage was already taking place:

> Complete salvage will probably require US submarine salvage ship *Pidgeon* (sic) now held in Manila. During withdrawal from Darwin of US ships with divers and deep water equipment no further preliminary diving can be effected with local resources.

Captain Gregory's second report, dated 1 February, 1942, is largely concerned with identification peculiarities of the submarine, perhaps for entry to identification records distributed to the fleet, and possible salvage of the submarine. Its detail is a tribute to the efficiency and skills of the divers:

> (d) The conning tower structure was reported to be about the size of those on our submarines on this station; the deck extends aft about 80 feet from the conning tower; there are three hatches abaft the conning tower spaced about 20 feet apart; the hatches are about 24" above the deck, the two after ones having streamlined fairwaters and appearing to be about 24" hatches but the one near the conning tower is not faired and is about 30" diameter.

> (e) At the starboard side of the conning tower there is a 24" hatch and outboard of that is a well in the deck extending for the length of the conning tower and bridge structure. There is no door in that side of the structure but a handhole cover was swung open displaying valves which may be the salvage air connections.

> (f) There is no radio antenna forward; the after antenna extends from the bridge structure to stanchions which are just forward of the after hatch.[a]

The report speculates on the condition of the submarine and possible raising. Small bubbles of air are reported, along with occasional oil bubble, and Gregory, presumably from discussion with Hawes, suggests that damage to the boat was slight, with the sinking perhaps resulting from "water taken in through the hatches". Part of a rubber gasket from one of the blown hatches, brought to the surface by the dive team, received considerable attention, with comparison to American versions and suggestions the Japanese design was "flimsy" and a "source of great weakness". Homer White, then a crewmember on the *USS Black Hawk*, remembers seeing the white rubber that sealed the gaskets, and he was in fact given a piece about six inches long,

---

a   The report uses the symbol " throughout to indicate inches – 12 inches = 30 cm. The radio antenna referred to in (f) is a wire leading from the bridge on the conning tower to one of the stern hatches.

which he kept for many years.[b]

Given that the depth charge damage was slight it is perhaps the case for the majority of the submarine's interior to be still watertight, with only some compartments flooded. The report gives brief attention to the possibilities of raising I-124:

> ...it is believed that the hull is intact...at each hatch there are two pad eyes and an air connection. The hatches could probably be made tight with lead gaskets and a strong-arm secured to the pad-eyes. Salvage is believed possible if suitable equipment were made available....Using the Pigeon the submarine might be blown light enough to be lifted and moved to shallow water, taking advantage of the large rise and fall of tide.

USS Pigeon, a submarine tender, had a primary mission, according to the Dictionary of American Naval Fighting Ships: "to salvage and aid submarines in distress". She carried full facilities for divers, and with her on the scene, I-124 could have been recovered. Pigeon was then in the Philippines, albeit to be one of several ships of the Asiatic Fleet trapped in the Manila Bay when the Americans surrendered Bataan and then Corredigor. Salvage without such resources at this early stage was obviously out of the question; indeed it is testimony to the determination of the American team that they did as well as they could, for the diving was deep, and fraught with operational difficulties:

> ...the Kookaburra had no air compressor, Holland's portable bank of air flasks were used and an unsatisfactory gasoline air compressor was borrowed from the Australian Army Command.

This is not to say some thought and indeed planning for recovery did not surround the wreck's codebooks; the next set of neap tides on 9 February was noted, and there was discussion – looked at later – at high levels about their recovery.

The Royal Australian Navy, however, certainly also thought the submarine might be worth entering, and immediately began the process of preparing for further dives. To do this, they planned to use the services of a famous salvage operator by the name of Captain John Williams, a man who was already well known. With his company, United Salvage, this intrepid adventurer had just finished commanding an operation that had salvaged a fortune in gold from SS Niagara off New Zealand.

This unfortunate ship had, in 1940, hit a mine laid by a German raider off the New Zealand

b   Navy diver Steve Cole suggested to the author that as the gasket on one hatch was "bulging" and the other was blown it may be the case that an internal explosion led to the hatch being open. Such an explosion would be perhaps linked to the depth charging, and be from chlorine gas (from the batteries) or diesel or both, but not an internal mine explosion, which would have destroyed the after half of the submarine.

coast some distance from Auckland's harbour. In *Gold from the Sea*, author JRW Taylor described how at a depth of 438 feet, using a diving bell, the Bank of England's gold had been successfully recovered from the sunken liner. Australian film-maker Jeff Maynard, who in the 1990s spent some considerable time researching additional material on the story, made a TV documentary – *Niagara's Gold* – on the subject. From his film[c] we can learn more of this daring adventurer and his team of divers and ship's crew.

On 19 June, 1940, the *Niagara*, (by strange coincidence Lieutenant Commander Menlove had once been one of her officers) an ocean liner and one-time World War I troopship, was taking eight tons of gold to America to pay for British armaments. Outside the harbour, she hit a mine and slowly sank, her crew and passengers all safely taking to the lifeboats in a calm sea, from which they were duly rescued. The British government, desperate for money, searched for a means of potential salvage. Captain John Williams came to their notice, and he was asked to take on the salvage attempt: finding the wreck, descending to the depths, and recovering the gold from a locked strongroom deep within the ship. To add to the problems, the ship was thought to be in depths well beyond the reach of any helmet diver.

Williams was more than equal to the task. He recruited a team of sailors and divers – the latter led by a diver who was to prove both fearless and resourceful, one "Johnno" Johnstone. The team also contained Captain James Hurd, a lifelong friend of Williams, and who was designated Chief Salvage Officer. Johnstone's brother Bill, who was a sailor in the RAN, was also seconded from the Navy for the task.

Williams was disadvantaged by the lack of a ship, all of the capable ones having been already taken up by the navies of Australia and New Zealand. Again he was equal to the task; finding an old abandoned hulk, the *Claymore*, in New Zealand, he rented it from the New Zealand government and set about renovating the old vessel. The wreck site was not known exactly; Williams took the *Claymore* to the approximate area and when the depth sounder would not work, resorted to dragging for the wreck with anchors, a dangerous task in an area known to be mined. The mines were certainly there – at one stage one was held off the *Claymore*'s hull by Johnno Johnstone in his dive suit – but the *Niagara* was seemingly not, and the search took a long time.

Eventually, when what seemed to be the shipwreck was located, Williams' and Johnstone's expertise combined. A diving bell had been obtained by this time, and work had been carried out on it to make it capable of descent to the previously unplumbed depths. On January 31, 1941, the anchor found something. Johnstone descended – and found the *Niagara* on her side.

Over the next months blasting operations were carried out to tear away the hull around the

---

c   *Niagara's Gold* was first screened on Australia's ABC-TV on 15 August 1996.

PAGE 102

strongroom. The diving bell would descend from the strongly braced *Claymore*, which was anchored to wooden buoys. The charges would be placed, and the bell would ascend and be hoisted out of the water. The charge would be set off, and then the bell would descend once more. The work was monotonous and dangerous, and often plagued by rough weather. Nevertheless, the team persisted, their labours only occasionally broken by some shore leave, where they established a reputation as determined drinkers. In October, the strongroom was opened, and after many attempts, the team's mechanical grab brought up a box with two gold bars inside.

Over the next two months, almost all of the rest of the gold was recovered. On December 7, the team left the wreck. Captain Williams was not to get much rest. From Melbourne he was sent to Singapore, but missed a connection in Brisbane for Darwin; the plane he should have been on was shot down off Koepang. His eventual arrival in Darwin was doubly opportune however, and a signal was made by southern commanders to the Naval Officer in Charge on 31 January:

> Understand Capt. Williams United Stevedoring Company in Darwin. Request you contact him regarding your 0358Z/30. Am in contact with Capt. Long[d] and present proposal is to send necessary gear overland to arrive Darwin Friday 13th February.

Captain Williams assessed the situation quickly. That same day the Navy was able to signal back:

> Your 0359 31st Captain Williams optimistic and anxious to start. Unless essential (sic) for himself proceed overseas request approval be given for his immediate return to Melbourne to supervise collection and despatch of equipment.

The Melbourne-based Commander Long, the Director of Naval Intelligence, was even more keen to get started. There was no need for Williams to return south; the equipment would be immediately sent north. Long advised of his intention to begin:

> ...despatching gear including explosive charges overland p.m. Monday 2nd. Request Williams concurrence and recommendation regarding gear despatched. Naval vessel will have to be used as diving tender.

Soon some of Williams' divers arrived in Darwin. Their arrival as civilians in the town preparing for war was not felicitous: the change in both climate and their status was a shock, according to Johnno Johnstone in his own manuscript "Wrecks was my Business":

---

d   This is curious: the chief of Naval Intelligence at the time – and indeed for the entire war – was Commander Long, not a Captain at any stage, although as Barbara Winter points out in *The Intrigue Master*, he was more than worthy of the rank.

...the heat was oppressive and although we had been warned, it was more than any of us could take. We had endured the icy cold winds of New Zealand for a year and so far survived; with the sudden change to over a 100 degrees in the shade, the sweat poured from us, even the tarmac burnt through one's shoes! Naval ratings in their spick and span white suits were everywhere; a few were waiting with a truck to meet us. The Naval Petty Officer in charge roared out "Now you fellows, listen to me!! You will load your gear and get aboard. We have a house ready for you and a meal at our mess – more than that, it is up to yourselves". It was easy to see the Navy had taken us over...[(p. 2)]

The men were confident of their ability, as well they might have been. They were there, according to their briefing, for an underwater inspection: "The Navy wanted a detailed examination and a report; if possible, photographs." The team, ensconced in its house, spent their days checking out boats and equipment – Williams' autobiography speaks of fitting out a "small cargo steamer" – and their evenings discussing both the possibility that Darwin would soon be bombed and the feasibility of raising the submarine. This was thought of as quite possible, and centred on the idea of making airhose connections to the hull, pumping in air and refloating *I-124*, in much the same manner as *HMS Thetis*, a British submarine, had recently been raised outside Liverpool in Britain.

Coming under the nominal command of the Navy, the *Niagara* team was a potential work force whose skills made them highly useful. While equipment was arriving from the south, there were plenty of small diving tasks around that could employ the team. One of these was the raising of a fuel barge, used for supplying fuel to the many Catalinas deployed from the port by the US Navy. On the morning of 19 February the team was assembled under the command of an American officer from the *USS William B. Preston*, a seaplane tender.[e] The team and a work party of 12 ratings from the tender went out for their dive in the local diesel workboat *Yampi Lass*.

Darwin resident Douglas Lockwood, writing in his 1966 book *Australia's Pearl Harbour*, described how the salvage attempt taking place in Darwin harbour was interrupted by the 10am Japanese raid:

When the raid began *Yampi Lass* was tending the well-known deep sea diver J.E.Johnstone, who had distinguished himself by recovering more than one million pounds of gold from the lost ship *Niagara* off the New Zealand coast. Johnstone was about to dive in an attempt to recover a sunken barge and had

---

[e] *USS William B. Preston* (AVD-7) was commanded temporarily by Lieutenant LO Wood, USN, on the morning of the attack, as her captain – Lieutenant Commander Etheridge Grant, USN – was ashore at the Naval Observers' Office. *Preston* was a converted destroyer of 1, 190 tons, with a flush deck and four funnels.

actually received the traditional "good luck" pat on the top of his helmet when the first bombs fell. He was on a ladder with his feet in the water when hauled back and his helmet removed. [p. 61]

Johnstone, however, differs a little. He says that he was actually on the seabed at a depth of 60 feet, without a telephone line rigged, when he felt himself:

> ...jerked off my feet, and I felt myself being pulled to the surface. Alf removed the helmet. "What's the big idea?" I asked him. "Come aboard and get the gear off quick. We are being bombed! Look at them over the town! They're in dozens! Bloody Japanese planes!!" I saw bombs dropping, they seemed to come from everywhere.

The American team left quickly on their launch. The *Preston* was to be both bombed and strafed, although she escaped the fate of her sister-destroyer, *USS Peary*. [f] This ship, anchored at the beginning of the raid, went down quickly, but fought all the way – many witnesses attest to the sight of the US sailors manning their guns to the last as the *Peary* sunk by the stern. The *William B. Preston* meanwhile, was also a primary target, as one of the bigger warships in the harbour. While her remaining three Catalina aircraft were destroyed at their moorings – her other two charges were respectively shot down near Melville Island and escaped to Groote Eylandt – the ship was effecting a high speed escape for the open sea and searoom. Attacking Japanese planes were to receive a nastier reception from this ship than they had been given from the *Peary* however. The *Preston* had several more machine guns mounted than did *Peary*; machine guns that had been destined for the Catalinas. Consequently several Japanese aircraft, making an attack on the destroyer as it fled the scene, were surprised by the intensity of the anti-aircraft fire that rose to meet them and pulled out of their dives.

Meanwhile Darwin was receiving the full impact of the force that had attacked Pearl Harbor in December 1941. The Japanese carriers had launched 188 aircraft to strike the town and the ships in the huge harbour. With only a flight of American Kittyhawks joining the shore and ships' anti-aircraft fire in defence, the destruction inflicted by the Japanese aircraft was immense. The official count lists 243 people killed – some accounts claim more[g] – and within the harbour eight ships were sunk, with another two lost outside in waters to the north.

Yampi Lass and the dive team received their share of attention from the attacking aircraft. The RAN crew on board zig-zagged the workboat towards shore at full power. Near the wharf the

---

f   *USS Peary* (DD 226), laid down in 1919, was commanded by Lieutenant Commander John M. Bermingham, USN. A sister-ship of *USS William B. Preston*, she was armed with four four-inch guns, one three inch gun, two .50 calibre machine guns and twelve 21 inch torpedo tubes in four triple mounts.

g   The same author's book *A War at Home* contains a list of those lost in action, which totals 251.

ammunition ship *Neptuna* was on fire, a railway engine had been blown off the wharf, and ships and boats were attempting to cast off their moorings, get under way and defend themselves against the wheeling aircraft, all at the same time. *Yampi Lass* was met by an air-force crash boat and directed to help take crews off sinking ships. Johnstone himself helped men from the *Admiral Halstead*, the decks of which he saw were piled high with drums of high-octane aviation fuel. As he was about to jump to the deck of the workboat one of the crew called out a plea to get the ship's dog. Johnstone ran back to the foc's'le, and found the dog, which promptly bit him when he picked it up. Johnstone dropped it over the side to the waiting arms below and jumped for the *Yampi Lass*.

Meanwhile, Williams had been caught on the wharf. One of his team, Arthur Bryant, had found a small boat and set out – backwards – to rescue those in the water; Williams tried to join him but the boat only had reverse gear and Bryant couldn't get back. Williams went back to the Boom Net yard but was forced by strafing aircraft to take shelter with others, incidentally where he had a good view of the *Peary* sinking. The harbour was covered with smoke from burning fuels; small boats were frantically being deployed to rescue men in the water, and over the whole scene the Japanese aircraft bombed and strafed, while below the defenders sent up a hail of lead from every gun that could be deployed on land and sea. *Deloraine* was one of the few warships to escape heavy damage or sinking; Lieutenant Commander Menlove recalled his cousin Alan Smith, third officer in the hospital ship *Manunda*, was killed in action, despite the red crosses prominently marking the ship.[1] The corvette *Katoomba* meanwhile, was in the rather unusual position of being in the floating dry dock – courtesy of her *Pecos* collision – and from there she put up a spirited fire, despite her odd predicament.

The departure of the Japanese aircraft meant a momentary lull in hostilities for the town, but two hours after the first raid land-based bombers struck the local airport, and Darwin became the scene of even more confusion. For the next six hours the Navy and dive team members continued their work of rescue on the harbour, while on shore the airport had been devastated and the town itself had been heavily damaged. The raid had brought home the once-distant war with grim reality.

After the attack Captain Williams was immediately employed as a temporary harbour pilot, helping ships get alongside the now shattered wharf. The divers were sent for again by the Navy; this time for a different task, as Johnstone relates:

> Seated at a table, was the Naval Officer in Charge, Commander Thomas. "Well Johnstone" he commenced, "you have a lot of work ahead of you. What can be done about getting these ships on their feet again? The sooner the better!"
>
> "I'm afraid sir, at present, not much. We haven't got the gear here for such work.

We'll need much more than is available in Australia! All we have with us is the observation bell we brought up with us. The job we came up here to do, was to survey the sunken Japanese submarine."

"In that case then, you're no b----y use up here" and with that, I was dismissed. (p. 10)

Johnstone spoke to Williams about the interview, and the Captain was not pleased. He met with Commander Thomas; Williams' view that the submarine should still be the focus prevailed, and soon Johnstone was despatched back to Melbourne, to return with all the salvage gear available. Williams soon followed. The gear was packed and again Johnstone departed for Darwin, but once there the views of a certain Captain John Faut prevailed, and as Johnstone concludes, "with the result that we got nowhere".[2]

Instead, the team was asked to check out the beached freighter *Don Isidro*, bombed by the Japanese on the fateful 19th, and now aground on Bathurst Island. Nothing in Johnstone's opinion was salvageable, but Faut's view prevailed again, and five weeks were spent trying to salvage the ship. Testimony to Johnstone's opinion can be seen today – the wreck of the *Don Isidro* is still beached, although little now remains: the ship was used as a target by the RAAF later in the war. Nor was the salvage of many of the harbour wrecks attempted; despite the undoubted fact that some of that work would have been both easy and fruitful. Instead the salvage team was employed on minor repairs: Lieutenant Frederick Purves RAN, (later a Rear-Admiral) remembers working on the beached *Port Mar* under the supervision of both Williams and Johnstone; Robert Rayner in *The Army and the Defence of Darwin Fortress* lists "eight 75mm guns plus jeeps and thirty two trucks" (p. 239) as being recovered, with all of the work being done under cover of darkness.

But this was not what Williams' team did best: the *Meigs*, for example, the biggest ship wrecked, was resting on the bottom with her masts and funnels above the water line, and the cargo of war equipment would have been a simple salvage to men with the *Niagara* team's skills. As it was only a few artillery pieces were recovered. Even some of the specialised salvage equipment brought to Darwin disappeared, and some time later Captain Williams embarked on legal action for its loss – a postscript to potential wasted.

(Endnotes)

1   Some controversy surrounds this attack: there have been suggestions it was accidental. Lieutenant (E) Frederick Purves, RANR(S), later Rear-Admiral RAN, with a clear view of *Manunda* from the deck of *Platypus*, witnessed the attack by a group of dive bombers. He is certain that this group acted in concert, and that the attack was deliberate. For him, the only uncertainty lies in the reason for the Japanese reluctance to sink, rather than merely disable, the hospital ship, the floating dock and *Platypus*. Alan Powell in *The Shadow's Edge* gives opinions from both sides. See also Rupert Goodman's *Hospital Ships*. Brisbane: Boolarong Publications, 1992.

2   Details on Faut are unknown. He is cited in Johnstone's own manuscript "Wrecks was my Business", as accompanying Johnstone on the return trip north: "John was a great fellow, but on salvage matters we differed..." (9) Johnstone notes that Faut was "Salvage Officer in Charge", but does not specify whether he was from Williams' company, RN, RAN or anything else. "Commander" Thomas was actually a captain.

One of the submarine squadron's mines on a Darwin beach. (Ron K Urquhart collection/NT Archives)

CHAPTER II

– BETWEEN SINKING AND SALVAGE

The successful sinking of the submarine eventuated in due rewards and recognition for *Deloraine* and her crew. Lieutenant Commander Menlove was admitted to the Distinguished Service Order for his command of the action, and Lieutenant Bruce Harvey was awarded the Distinguished Service Cross: "...for skill and resource in *HMAS Deloraine* when the Japanese submarine I124 was destroyed off Darwin on 21 January, 1942." This same wording was also used in recognising the following crew members, two of whom received the Distinguished Service Medal, while the others received the Mentioned In Dispatches honour. (This has fallen into disuse in most forces today, but in WWII was recognised with an oak leaf badge worn on another medal.)

- Savage, Frederick James, Leading Seaman, Distinguished Service Medal;

- Taite, Carson Jefferson, Able Seaman, Distinguished Service Medal;

- Crisp, Arthur Bernard, Petty Officer Stoker, Mentioned In Dispatches;

- Ctercteko, William David, Chief Engineroom
  Artificer, Mentioned In Dispatches;

- Graham, Kenneth Arthur, Engineer Lieutenant,
  RANR(S), Mentioned In Dispatches;

- O'Neill, Horace William Peter, Able Seaman, Mentioned In Dispatches;

- Rogan, Clarrie Joseph, Stoker, Mentioned In Dispatches.[1]

Deloraine hardly paused for breath before being involved in further action. There is an interesting possibility that the carrier force was seen from the corvette before the Darwin strike from the incoming Japanese carrier force, which cements the ship's status as being extremely lucky, notwithstanding the undoubted skill of her crew. Dan Studeman, writing in his book *A Small War*, recalled during his time in *Deloraine* a sighting of the Japanese carriers before they attacked:

Smith Street, Darwin, some time after the initial air raids, with damage evident to Cashman's Newsagency and the Bank of New South Wales next door. In the background is the Commonwealth Bank. All three buildings can still be seen in what is now the Darwin Mall today. (Historical Repository, HMAS Coonawarra, Darwin)

About 1800 hours on 17th February, 1942 the ship was in the Arafura Sea, about 12 hours out of Darwin[2], heading into heavy seas left by the tail of a cyclone, it was raining heavily and visibility was extremely poor, the signalman on bridge spoke down to his mate in the wireless room, "Hey Buster, go outside and have a squiz". Buster went out to the port waist and, during a small break in the weather an aircraft carrier, escorted by a cruiser was clearly visible, with the smoke of more ships easily seen further back. Buster wasn't too sure if the ships were Japanese but felt they weren't American and he knew they couldn't be Australian. After reporting to the officer of the watch, Norm McK., the signalman gave the carrier the three blink challenge asking its identity, what he received back was a steady flashing which couldn't interpret (sic). Other men were taking a breather in the starboard waist and some began pointing to sea an angle of 35° aft. The LTO on depth charge watch also observed the menacing sight, confirming that no one was dreaming, or seeing ghosts. The sightings were of an aircraft carrier and another capital ship and, much smoke was seen below the horizon. The weather closed in again and nothing further was seen of the ships. *Deloraine* and *Admiral Halstead* proceeded to Darwin where Commander Menlove was landed suffering acute Dengue Fever. The big question will never be answered, had *Deloraine* broken radio silence and spoken to Darwin would that warning have saved Darwin from the devastation to come? Had the ship signalled Darwin it is certain she would have been engaged and sunk without trace...[p. 11-12]

I-124's sister boats withdrew from the area, and eventually the news of the loss of their companion submarine and Squadron Commander Endo would have confirmed *I-123*'s suspicions and confirmed to *I-121* that she had not missed *I-124* in a January-end rendezvous. American cryptoanalysts picked up a message from the Southern Area Subforce Commander on the 30th: "The *I-121* arrived at scheduled rendezvous.....at the appointed time from 0600/28 until 0000/29 January but failing to sight or hear from the *I-124* it started out alone on the return trip."

The three remaining boats of the squadron then departed for northern waters, returning to their base ship in the Philippines. However, the three boats soon returned to Australian waters. *I-121* returned to a position 50 miles northwest of Darwin (not far from *I-124*'s resting place) and acted as a weather reporting vessel for the massive carrier raid on Darwin on 19th February. Meanwhile *I-122* had returned to patrol off Torres Strait, apparently without result. *I-123* had also been ordered to Torres Strait and laid 40 mines there on 23rd February: there is no record of these mines doing any damage. Soon after all three boats rejoined their base ship and returned to Japan. None would return to Australian waters. *I-121* was the only boat to survive the war; *I-123* was sunk by the destroyer-minelayer *USS Gamble* to the east of Savo Island in the Solomons in August 1942, and *I-122* was sunk by the American submarine *USS Skate* in June 1945. *I-121* was scuttled by occupation forces.[3]

I-124 was not the subject of any continuing stories about its demise within the port of Darwin, indeed its very presence seems to have been unknown to many of the thousands of sailors passing through the town or stationed there to defend it. Lieutenant Harold Morris, for example, now living in Tasmania, was posted in mid-1942 to Darwin, an air journey that took him two days via East-West airlines. Once in the port that had so recently been attacked he boarded the patrol boat *Vigilant*, only to find that it was condemned as unseaworthy shortly afterwards. With little time ashore in the port of Darwin he was posted to *HMAS Kuru*.

Lieutenant Morris participated in several voyages to Timor, where the beleaguered commandos of Sparrow Force were relying so heavily on the Navy. Later he commanded his own vessel *Kiara*, working around Darwin to patrol the harbour's boom net and surrounding waters. Despite this extensive work within the area, he recalls only occasional comment about *I-124*.

Similarly Lieutenant Commander John "Lucky" Ross[a], an officer who served in *HMAS Sydney*; escaped death in *HMAS Canberra* and was posted to Darwin at the end of the war, remembers:

> Regarding *I-124*, I am surprised, looking back, that we knew nothing about it at Darwin in '46/7. I cannot recall that there was ever any mention of it in the Mess or in the town itself, and I feel confident that if any of our personnel had any information about it there would have been a lot of discussion and that I would still recall it. It appears therefore, that the aftermath of the sinking was, at that stage, very "hush-hush".

This was not to prevent the beginning of the many myths that surround the submarine, however. One story from Owen Griffiths' book *Darwin Drama* tells an occasion during the war when *HMAS Warrnambool* supposedly obtained a load of fresh fish courtesy of *I-124*. The corvette, it is suggested, was carrying out exercises on the sunken submarine and had dropped a depth charge on it. The book goes on:

> From two to two and a half tons of red morwong of 11 lbs. weight each came floating to the surface together with two coral cod, each 500 lb. weight. On gutting some of the fish they were found to contain rice which had obviously come from the Jap submarine lying on the ocean bed. The decks of *Warrnambool* were laden with the precious food and there was sufficient for the whole of the Darwin Navy.
> (p. 123)

Lieutenant Morris's wry comment on this story is that he "hadn't heard that one...."

Dan Studeman also suggests that in 1944 *HMAS Shepparton* launched an attack on a submarine in the same area. "Air bubbles, oily slicks and flotsam were noted but no submarine surfaced. Reporting the attack to Darwin, *Shepparton* was told they had killed a "dead" submarine, ie, *Deloraine* victim." [(p. 37)] Curiously, according to crewman Jack Valli, *Shepparton* launched her attack when two torpedo tracks were seen just to miss the corvette and consequently asdic gained a contact. Jack Valli claimed, after the war, a German submarine was understood to be in the area.[b]

Whether the minelaying squadron's mines were responsible for sinking any more shipping is not clear. Mines were reported in the area on 28 and 29 January, and also in early February. On

---

a   John Ross's autobiography *Lucky Ross* recounts his remarkable adventures in a very readable form.

b   Naval Historian David Stevens, specialising in the history of enemy submarines in Australian waters, comments: "Definitely no German submarines in Darwin area. They are all fully accounted for. No Japanese that I am aware of" and confirms in his essay "South-West Pacific Sea Frontiers" that: "the Japanese had ceased submarine operations against Australia in July 1943" (97). He also meticulously details the German deployments, noting four U-boats assigned to the area in late 1944, with three out of four sunk shortly after the embarkation. No U-boats were deployed to the area in early 1944. In fact, Stevens points out the knowledge of this was so certain the convoy system south of Townsville was abolished in February.

11 February a party led by a Lieutenant Croft took *Vigilant* to four mines washed up on a beach at Gunn Point, outside Darwin's harbour.[c] The mines were rendered safe, and according to the 1942 *HMAS Melville* report one was "brought back to Darwin as a specimen". Iris Nesdale suggests in *Small Ships at War* that the mine was eventually taken to Flinders Naval Depot for examination; there is certainly now one of the squadron's mines at the Clearance Divers' Museum in *HMAS Penguin*.

The author JE McDonnell used the submarine sinking as the basis for a short chapter in his book *As You Were*, published in 1948. There the sinking of *I-124* is described from the viewpoint of a

(two photographs above) Deloraine crewmembers during 1942. (Bill Hornery)

c   These may have come from *I-123*. Her war diary says she laid 30 mines in Dundas Strait at 1916 on the 20th Jan.

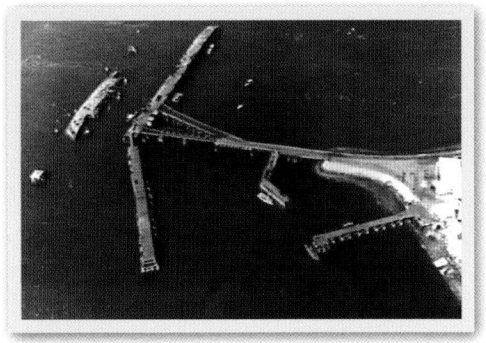

Part of Darwin Harbour in 1943. The wreck of the Neptuna can be clearly seen – one of the wrecks which was to inconvenience shipping for the next 16 years. (Historical Repository, HMAS Coonawarra, Darwin)

crewman in an unnamed warship. *Deloraine* is described in dramatic terms:

> The corvette nosed down her asdic beam like a bloodhound on the trail, a white cloud of foam opening at her bows....on the quarterdeck the depth charge crews were throwing them overboard like chicken feed....squeezing the submarine's plates with the force of a mighty steam hammer...inside her a shower of cork shook from the deckhead. Brass fittings, switch covers were jerked loose and flung across the room under the blast. One Jap on the control panel uttered a sudden cry of pain...the captain dived still deeper....Soon it came - an oil slick seeping up like a gout of blood from the pressured depths. A current slid it down wind and we smelt its pungent reek, "made in Japan". That was sufficient. The senior ship draped herself in congratulatory flags, and leaving *Deloraine* sniffing round her dead foe the rest of us coursed home for Darwin's boom. [(p. 125-6)]

The sinking of the submarine was also the subject for a radio play. The Australian Broadcasting Commission (as the ABC was called then) had a field unit in Darwin during 1942. Written by a Peter Hemery, the radio play: "Death of a Sub", was sent to the ABC's Sydney-based Federal Controller of Talks on 29 May 1942. The letter accompanying the "two discs" on which the play was recorded, specifies, however, that the play material is of a secret nature:

> I am forwarding under safe hand through Navy Office two discs PH45/46 "Death of a Sub". These recordings, as you will see from perusal of the script, contain a story which can only be released at the discretion of Navy Board, and we have made the broadcast for future release and historical record only. Navy has asked us to use the greatest care in seeing that these recordings and all documents pertaining to them are treated with the utmost secrecy.

> The records were made under the closest Naval supervision, and have been auditioned to and approved by the Commodore and Intelligence Officer of this area.

In spite of our best endeavours, we were unable to record depth charges, the recorder lifting gently and coming to earth some seconds later; so that these effects will have to be dubbed in...

The play itself contained dramatic dialogue, although curiously the ship featured as sinking *I-124* was *Lithgow*:

HEMERY. No sooner had one attack been made than the little minesweeper had turned on her heel, listing with her speed, and was dashing back again at the guidance of the imperious, monotonous call of her location gear.

ESTABLISH ASDIC BACKGROUND BRIEFLY
Suddenly a silence which seemed to roar by comparison with the endless pinging of the "Asdic" focussed every eye on the startled "Asdic" operator, as the micro-adjusted gear failed owing to the pounding of the depth charges...

RE-ESTABLISH ASDIC, STOP ON CUE

COMMANDER. What is it, Sub....What's happened?

SUB. Asdic failed, sir....Must have been the charges....I'll investigate at once.

HEMERY. Lucky was "*Lithgow*". For at that moment, after the third attack, the crippled submarine attempted to surface. Either she was so badly crippled that

Desmond Menlove kept well out of debates over his defeated enemy. He died in 1990, after a long and successful life. (Jean Menlove)

Atsuko Kishigami with local Customs official Junnosuke Sumida, and Western merchant Charles Ryder, studying a 1940s photo of Darwin. (Atsuko Kishigami)

her commander had decided to surrender, or else it was an unsuccessful attempt to fight from the surface, using her torpedo tubes and deck armament. As the sub. rose, "*Lithgow*" prepared to give her a fitting welcome....

LOOKOUT. (THROUGH SPEAKING TUBE) Broken water on the port quarter sir

COMMANDER. By Jove...I think she's trying to surface...Stand by gun crew..

GUNNERY OFFICER. (Passes range to gun.)

COMMANDER. It's the only thing it could be...Look at the shape of the disturbed patch...longer than our ship and narrow...It's exactly abeam...Must be a big one...

OFFICER OF THE WATCH. We must have hit her, sir...Look at the oil, and those huge air bubbles...

COMMANDER. Not a doubt of it...Look...You can see the water parting in the middle...There's nothing else would displace water like that...We'll give her a few more charges...(FADING) Just to make sure of her...She's probably still got some fight left.

HEMERY. Fair in the middle of the long, narrow, strip of churning tormented water landed "*Lithgow*'s" accurately flung charges. When the tornado of water had subsided, a six inch scum of oil moved uneasily; great bubbles of air turned iridescent by the oil glopped through it. A few scattered pieces of torn debris floated like a funeral wreathe above the submarine's grave.

The "asdic" gear, now working again, held the submarine...but this time there was no movement. The first submarine to be killed in Australian waters had received its death blow. Divers investigating later found that "*Lithgow*'s" aim had been true. Her conning tower had been blown clean off, and two hatches had been forced open, allowing floods of water into the stricken sub's hull.

Whether the play was ever broadcast or not is unclear. Despite a diligent search by Sydney ABC archivist Guy Tranter, there is as of yet no record found which indicates a broadcast date. However, there is reason to think that "Death of a Sub" never made it to air. In a letter dated 22 June 1942 an ABC officer informs Hemery, amongst other details of scripts, broadcasts and the like, that: "Discs 45, 46, 47 - I have already informed you that the naval authorities after passing these recordings to Mr Nicholls almost immediately recalled them."

As to whether the discs were ever returned to the ABC, or whether a broadcast or broadcasts were ever made has not yet been determined.

Deloraine's crew served with distinction during the war and beyond its end in 1945. Gunnery Officer Eric Thompson became the First Lieutenant of *Deloraine* and commanded her briefly in November 1944. Thompson was one of the crew who stayed in the Navy after the end of the war. He was promoted to Lieutenant Commander and retired from full-time service in 1958, but served for many years as the commander of Cadet Training Ship *Tamar*, and was later the Senior Officer of the Tasmanian Division.

Desmond Menlove continued to serve on various ships for the rest of the war, including both shore and sea postings. In 1944, when he celebrated the birth of another son, Christopher; he was commended for his command of *HMAS Manoora*, an infantry landing ship, during the embarkation of assault troops into their boats during the attack on Wadke Island, off New Guinea. After the war he went back to the Merchant Navy and joined the Torres Strait Pilot Service. Separating from Marion, Menlove re-married to a new wife, Jean. When his 35th year at sea was completed, Menlove resigned and began a new career in insurance. He was highly successful there too: being the first insurance representative in NSW to write a million dollar policy, and handling an immense amount of business, due largely, according to others, because of the trust people placed in him. He also seems to have been a witty and humourous man, who liked to tell stories to company. His private life was largely devoid of hobbies though; when queried on this Menlove always gave "work" as his major hobby. He died in 1990.

The memorable Carl Atkinson – contracted to assess the I-124 salvage. The ship's wheel he is leaning on is from the USS Peary, and is now displayed in the Australian National Maritime Museum in Sydney. (Cherry Perron)

HMAS Deloraine went on to a distinguished career, becoming the most decorated corvette of the 56 in the RAN. In January 1943, now under the command of Lieutenant Commander C. Weston, she went into action against another Japanese submarine - *I-21* - which had torpedoed an American freighter, the *Peter H Burnett*, some 420 miles east of Sydney. The Japanese submarine had disappeared before ensuring her target was properly sinking, and the freighter was still afloat. Joined by three other ships, *Deloraine* took the crippled ship in tow and brought her safely into Sydney.

A few months later the corvette again rescued survivors from another Japanese submarine's target: this time it was *I-177* which had torpedoed a Liberty ship east of Newcastle. *Deloraine* recovered 62 survivors. In June 1943 she again rescued survivors after the submarine *I-174* attacked a convoy *Deloraine* was helping escort. The success of the *I-124* action was not repeated for the other corvettes however, and *I-174* made good her escape. In 1944 and 1945 *Deloraine* operated in New Guinea waters in a variety of roles, including that of shore bombardment.

In June 1948 the corvette paid off into reserve, and in 1956 was sold to the Delta Shipping Company of Hong Kong for breaking up. The ship is commemorated by the *HMAS Deloraine* Trophy, donated to the RAN by Thorn EMI Electronics. This is presented annually at the Surface Warfare School in *HMAS Watson* – a Sydney shore base – to the dux of the sailors' warfare course held there. Originally donated to the School in 1988, the trophy's initial ceremony of presentation was attended by five members of the corvette's crew at the time of the *I-124* sinking: Daniel Studeman, Ralph Mortimer, Desmond Menlove, Fred Savage and Stanley Hale. The trophy may still be seen by visitors to the school, displayed proudly in the main foyer.

In the late 1950s Commander Kishigami's eldest daughter, Atsuko Kishigami, living in the small town of Tanabe with her mother Fusae and her younger sister Etsuko, became interested in finding out exactly where her father's submarine was sunk. She turned for help to the local Customs Officer, Junnosuke Sumida, and he in turn contacted a local British trader, Charles Ryder. Ryder asked the Qantas airline for a photograph of Darwin, which was duly provided – Mrs Kishigami still has the photograph, showing the city in the late 1940s, and with a significant cross marked within the harbour. Featured in the local newspaper, Atsuko is pictured gazing at the photograph, while Charles Ryder and the Customs official look on. The photograph, and the thought of her father's submarine lying in foreign waters, had an effect on Atsuko Kishigami which was to last for decades.

In July 1958 Kishigami's daughter began a campaign to have the submarine entered or raised, and the remains of the crew returned to Japan. Other relatives of the submarine's crew were contacted, and Atsuko began to act as a focal point for letters of support to the Japanese government proposing the submarine be raised.

Some of this may have been motivated by religious feelings. In March each year the Japanese hold a festival in which the spirits of the dead are said to return briefly to visit the living relatives. For the spirit to be truly happy, the bodily remains must be within the Home Islands of Japan.

Soon a letter was composed to the Japanese Prime Minister, the Foreign Minister, and the Minister for Welfare. By this time, it was learnt that the Fujita Salvage Company had arrived in Darwin. The Company had tendered successfully to remove the wrecks littering Darwin Harbour, which ironically had been sunk there years before by the Japanese armed forces. Although it might have been expected that given the nationality of the salvors there might have been opposition within the city for the operation, there was in fact very little. Several companies had tendered in previous years to remove the wrecks, which were obstructing shipping – *Neptuna*'s wreck still lay on its side next to the wharf, and *Meigs*' topmasts and

An article from a 1958 Japanese newspaper, outlining the quest Atsuko Kishigami began. (Atsuko Kishigami)

funnels could be seen at low tide, while others were enough of an obstruction to have been marked with buoys and flashing lights. The previously contracted companies had without exception failed to deliver, and the only salvage was done by local larger-than-life identity Carl Atkinson.

Operating from Doctor's Gully (where the fish-feeding tourist attraction, Aquascene, is now located) Atkinson had in fact bought some of the wrecks, and was often engaged in raising various items from them. When the local Customs objected to some of the items that had been brought to the surface, some light trucks, for example, claiming that they were dutiable, Atkinson simply dived at night to avoid detection. He had also raised various items from the *USS Peary*, which had gone down fighting offshore on 19 February 1942, including the ship's wheel, which is now displayed in the Australian National Maritime Museum in Sydney.[d]

Mrs Kishigami remembers Carl Atkinson was contracted to search for the submarine, even though it was well outside the harbour where Fujita Salvage and Atkinson normally operated. A resourceful and fearless diver, Atkinson did what was asked of him, and it seems duly reported to Fujita Salvage the submarine's location and condition, so an assessment could be made for raising. Interestingly, this hints at a co-operation between Atkinson and Fujita Salvage that was not always obvious, at least as far as the media was concerned. Atkinson had been in several rows over the sale of his wrecks. Later, his co-operation disappeared entirely, when negotiations between Fujita Salvage and himself broke down over the sale of the destroyer *USS Peary*.

Eventually the Japanese raised completely the tanker *British Motorist*. Most of the upper hulls of *Meigs* and *Mauna Loa* were raised, although their hulls from the Plimsoll line down remain complete with cargo, and much of *Zealandia* and almost all of the *Peary*. However, the salvage of *I-124* did not proceed.

The reason for this seems to have been the cost involved. The depth of the wreck, its distance from land facilities, and the open sea and the associated rough weather which would have hampered salvage operations all combined to add massively to the cost of raising the submarine. However, it does appear that a trip was made with some secrecy to the wreck site. The Harbourmaster, BL Noble, made a voyage on one of Fujita's salvage vessels, the *Nachi Maru*, although he was mystified as to its purpose:

> Embarked aboard vessel 0315 hours 10th August, proceeding immediately to sea with salvage workboat in tow. En route, the latter vessel suffered the loss of her rudder necessitating emergency repairs, which were carried out without causing any delay.

---

d   Darwin diver and wreck historian Phil Franklin uncovered another interesting story about Atkinson. Apparently at one time his girlfriend was surprised whilst ironing a large pile of damp banknotes.

We arrived at a position 3 miles West of Point Fourcroy light at 1530 hours August 10th and proceeded coastwise to a position 3 miles south of Malgrew Point...the wreck in which the Japanese have shown interest was said to lie in 4 fathoms of water 1&1/2 miles inshore from the latter position. However, as no portion of the wreck was visible, a fact with which they had been acquainted prior to leaving Darwin, they showed little interest in the matter, and the vessel and her tow proceeded on the return voyage at 1630 hours....

While off Bathurst Island the Japanese showed no inclination and made no attempt to land thereon.

The purpose of the voyage appears to be obscure and my surprise, when no real interest was shown in the wreck, was met with oriental inscrutability.

The track of this short voyage took the two vessels over the area in which *I-124* lay. With a simple depth sounder operating en route, the Japanese would have been able to gain a good indication of the sea depth in the wreck area, even if their track did not take them directly over the wreck, and also of the distance they would have been required to operate from land. They therefore gained by this simple voyage some idea of the complexity of a possible salvage.

The 1950s attention was publicised in the early 1970s, when the submarine was to become the focus of a real salvage attempt. Journalist Gavin Souter claimed in two 1973 articles, published in *The Australian* and *The Sun* newspapers, that an attempt was made in 1958 to recover human remains from *I-124*. He appears to have had some contact with the Japanese Embassy, who confirmed the story:

> One of the prime movers was Commander Kishigami's eldest daughter, Atsuko Kishigami. "The families wanted to collect the remains," says the press attache at the Japanese Embassy in Canberra, Mr M Okubo. "It was very understandable. The Australian Minister for External Affairs, Mr Casey, was favourable. But it turned out that it would cost too much to float." [(p. 15)]

However, the Japanese Embassy was unable to confirm this story in 1995, stating that "...as we do not have any records from the 1950s, we cannot, verify or trace any further information relating to this matter."

This story was however, known to later salvage groups of the 1970s, who wanted to recover the submarine. In discussions originating from lawyers acting for a potential salvage group, it was stated that: "...the daughter of the submarine's captain is still alive and resident in Tokyo and that she has been the main agitator since the end of the war for the return of the bodies to

Fujita salvage divers at work in Darwin harbour. (Northern Territory Library)

Japan." And further:

> It is believed that the Fujita salvaging Company (sic) working on the shipping in
> the Port Darwin area after the war, might have confirmed the existence of the
> submarine off Bathurst Island and that the next of kin of the deceased on the
> submarine had asked the government at that time for the corpses to be recovered,
> but because of the cost the Government shelved the proposal....One thing is very
> clear and that is the next of kin wish to recover the corpses and that they have
> brough (sic) pressure on the Japanese Government from apparently about the
> time of the conclusion of the war to this end.

The submarine, if not visited, certainly was in the thoughts of the local diving community. In
the 1960s, it must be borne in mind, scuba diving as we know it today was largely unknown,
and a dangerous sport in the minds of the general public, reinforced by the daredevil image
of divers such as Buster Crabbe and fictional counterparts. Safety was not the overriding
concern it is today, and many divers only dimly understood the physics and chemistry that
underpins diving. Failure to understand these disciplines can lead to incurring serious injury
while underwater: burst eardrums, decompression sickness (the "bends"), lung injuries, and if
unfortunate, death by drowning.

Notwithstanding all of this, the local divers certainly considered *I-124* as being the dive of a
lifetime. Perhaps fortunately for them, considering its depth, the wreck site was only vaguely

Darwin in 1958. The wharf – with its attendant Neptuna – is off to the left of this picture. HMAS Melville, one of the Navy's two shore bases, was made up partly of the long buildings in the background; the Northern Territory's Parliament House and Supreme Court are in this position now. To the right, just below the water tower, is Smith Street, where Darwin's mall is now located. The Bank of New South Wales and the Commonwealth Bank building, which still look the same today, can be seen on the corner. In the foreground was once located "Chinatown" – bombed and burnt and eventually bulldozed in the war. In the foreground of this fascinating photograph is HMAS Sydney, one of the RAN's two aircraft carriers of the period. (Historical Repository, HMAS Coonawarra, Darwin)

known. Marshall Perron, later to become the Chief Minister of the Northern Territory, recalls that they talked of the *Don Isidro*, the *Florence D*, and the submarine as all being worth seeking out. The *Don Isidro* and *Florence D* were both small ships which were unfortunate enough to be in the area when the Japanese aircraft swooped down on Darwin that disastrous day of 19 February, 1942. The two freighters, just like eight ships inside the harbour, were sunk by bombs and strafing. The *Don Isidro* ran aground off Cape Fourcroy , and the *Florence D* was only found in the late 1990s, despite the bearings taken by Lieutenant Tom Moorer USN (later Admiral), who was on board when it was attacked, having himself been shot down in his Catalina earlier in the day and picked up by the freighter.

While the Darwin divers of the 1960s found the *Don Isidro*'s remains, half under water on a beach, they decided *I-124* was too deep for them to try. "We were all terrified of narcosis,"

Marshall Perron recalls, and fellow diver Warren Allen agrees, adding that "the mercury story" (to be discussed later) was vaguely in the background too. However, for these two members of the original diving community in the Top End, their dismissal of *I-124* was to be forgotten in later years, when the submarine wreck reclaimed their attention in plans to dive and raise the wreck.

(Endnotes)

1   ¹ A full listing of honours and awards made in the RAN can be found in Atkinson's *By Skill and Valour*.

2   ² Crewman Len Crabbe contends the *Deloraine* was in fact 24 hours out of Darwin.

3   Imperial Japanese Navy Page. http://www.combinedfleet.com/I-121.htm - and other boat numbers for the two remaining. Accessed September 2010.

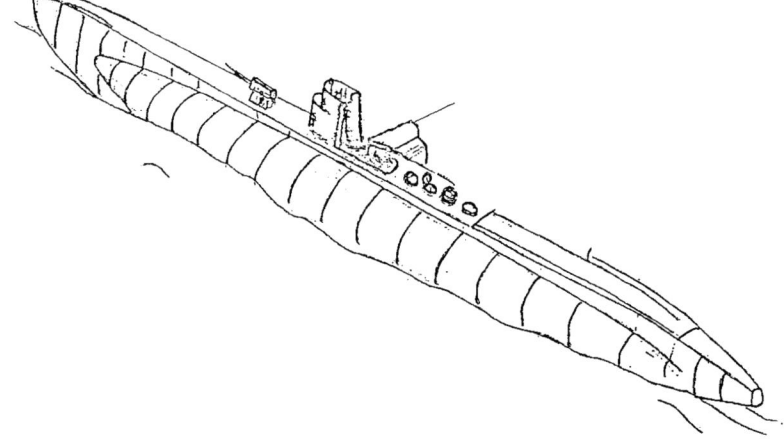

Chapter 12

– THE 1970S AND SALVAGE ATTEMPTS

In July 1972 salvage operators CJ (Sid) Hawks, Harry Baxter, and John Chadderton began preliminary salvage work on recovering *I-124*. The organisation of the three men took the form of a loose partnership. Harry Baxter was an NT-based salvage diver who carried out a miscellany of diving operations, and Sid Hawks and Johnny Chadderton were local workboat operators.

The exact location of the submarine was of first concern; while it was marked on some charts the precise position seems not to have been known to the three. Baxter, logically enough, asked the Royal Australian Navy if they knew of the location of their wartime kill. Lieutenant (later Commander) Ian Gibson, then in command of the *Attack* class patrol boat *HMAS Assail*, recalls Baxter asking for information: "Our patrol boats were moored at Stokes Hill, and Baxter was always around".

The plan, as formulated by Chadderton and Hawks, was to tie bulk cement tanks, obtained from a local company, to the hull of the submarine and then fill the tanks full of air, in order to refloat the vessel. Some planning as to what to do with *I-124* once she had been raised had been done, and Chadderton recalls being motivated by a story he had seen of a U-boat being toured around American towns. Preliminary planning, in any event, indicated that the submarine could be worth a lot of money.

The three men were an interesting band. They were all experienced in the ways of the sea and had led colourful lives.

Hawks[1], born in 1907 in Belfast, had trained as a marine engineer before his arrival in Australia in time for World War II. Although he had learnt to fly, he spent the duration in the RAAF as a Flight-Sergeant fitter, seeing service in a number of locations, including Townsville and Darwin. After the war he and his wife had spent some time in Brisbane setting up a textiles factory before arriving in Darwin, which Hawks recalls being told during the war would be a growing city. After some time as a station-owner, and store owner - of "Top Springs Store" – Hawks fell out with his wife, whose accounting practices, he said, were somewhat unconventional. He

Sid Hawks in his RAAF uniform in WWII. (Sid Hawks)

returned to the sea in 1959, working as an engineer in the Pacific, and buying the workboat *Larrapan* in the 1960s upon his return to Darwin, later selling it and buying the 17 metre steel workboat *Arandel*.

Baxter operated a commercial diving concern in Darwin. A former RAAF mechanic, Baxter was a colourful figure, professing – according to people who knew him – a dislike for "the Establishment" and its workings, although he was not above accepting the occasional diving job from the government. In one of his own advertisements, placed in the *Northern Territory News*, he described himself as "...diving in Darwin waters professionally since 1958". Darwin resident Jim Porter worked for him as a diver in the late 1960s on a casual basis, doing hull scrubs and the occasional deeper dive to place drill tips for harbour mining experiments. The Baxter organisation, Porter remembers, operated almost solely on hookah operations, whereby a diver was supplied via an air tube from the surface. Air bottles for scuba diving were often aboard Baxter's boat, but seemed rarely if ever used.

Chadderton was another figure who led a varied life. Born in 1950 in Mornington, Victoria, Chadderton had started off his work life as a jackaroo, but soon gave that up for a life at sea, which he candidly admits offered a lot more money. Learning to scuba dive and spearfish at an early age, he also distinguished himself as a youngster by skippering his first boat – a 32 foot fishing vessel – at the age of 15. Ferrying explosives to the Bass Strait oil rigs followed, and then

Chadderton moved onto bigger and better fishing vessels, eventually bringing the first prawn trawler to the Territory in the late 60s. He then bought the *Larrapan* from Hawks and was running a business supplying the isolated missions around the NT coastline. Like Hawks he had heard of *I-124* and began planning a mission to find it. Harry Baxter, both Chadderton and Hawks say, was bought in as a diver.

On Sunday 5 November, 1972, Lieutenant Gibson was commanding *Assail*, and having two hours before they could enter port, he decided to do some depth sounder runs over the site where the submarine was supposed to be located. After some time the wreck was located at a depth of 150 feet, rising some 50 feet at its highest point. This was mentioned to Baxter upon the *Assail*'s return.

On November 15, *Assail* was due to depart Darwin for patrol duty again, and in the meantime, Baxter had asked Lieutenant Gibson to buoy the site. Arriving, according to radar fix, at the site, *Assail*'s depth-sounder was unable to locate the wreck again.[2] However, a small dan-buoy was thrown over as close to the radar fix as possible. As *Assail* was ready to leave, a boat with Baxter on board arrived; the two vessels manoeuvred so they were close to each other, and the location progress was passed. *Assail* then departed.

Using the small vessels *Arnhem*[3] *T*, *Larrapan* and *Mutiara* the trio of potential salvors experienced some confusion in locating the wreck during their exploratory dives. Later in the day, however, having found the submarine, on 15 November 1972, they began dives and prepared for salvage.

Sid Hawks and John Chadderton in early 1996. Chadderton was still working at sea at the time, while Hawks – almost 90 – was retired. (author)

Once the three had found the submarine Baxter wrote a two page report on these first descents. He stated that after discovering *I-124*:

> We made two dives in a cage because there were many sharks in the area. On the second dive, just on dusk, another diver and I discovered the submarine.... We inspected the submarine at first light the next morning and discovered one open hatch. Inside the hatch were the bones of a Japanese crewman who had apparently tried to escape; there was escape apparatus in the form of oxygen bottles and a harness lying on the deck. There was a small hole in the lower half of the Conning Tower which seemed to have been made by a depth charge. We were unable to gain access to the submarine due to the hatch opening being made for Japanese seamen and being too small for us....I have inspected the submarine five times altogether. There is a 10 ft. shark which is always in the Conning Tower. The Conning Tower also contains a great deal of pearl shell. The submarine is surrounded by sharks, many man-eating gropers and sea snakes which seem to make it their home....It has light armament on the deck consisting of 5.5 gun and what appears to be some machine guns. The torpedo tubes were open and appeared to have been fired prior to the submarine being sunk.

However, according to Chadderton's report, when the submarine was located "the anchor chain of one vessel (*Mutiara*) had become entangled on the submarine, we used this to make our first and following dives." He then says, hinting at the division which was to affect the operation later:

> Baxter and one of his divers, Ray, made the first dive in a mesh cage to keep the sharks away. But when the cage was lowered only about 60 feet they indicated to stop and return to the surface. When the cage was winched up only Baxter was inside. He had apparently been scared by the sharks he saw. Ray had left the cage and carried on down the anchor chain to the submarine and swam from the bow to the conning tower....The next few days were taken up with further dives by myself and Ray....The sharks are no great problem even though there are probably 30 or 40 cruising around down to 70 feet....I found the submarine to be in perfect condition with only light growth from half way up the side of the hull over the deck and on the conning tower. The aft deck has 2 rows of petrol drums in brackets, which are intact.

There are many instances in Baxter's account which must cast doubt on his statements in total, hinting at either a lack of knowledge or a desire to sensationalise. The open hatch was the subject of particular scrutiny by the USN divers in 1942; they would surely have seen any "oxygen bottles", which *I-124* in any event probably would not have carried as escape kit. The hatches on *I-124* are not too small for a scuba diver, who is much less encumbered than a helmet diver and furthermore can remove a scuba tank and fins if necessary to get inside something – the author has done this to sit in a sunken Catalina's cockpit. Bones exposed to open sea quickly disappear: *Peary*'s wreck when discovered 14 years after her sinking had only a thigh bone found as remains of her 91 fatalities. Sea snakes are almost unknown in NT waters; the wreck of the *Marchart 3* a small distance to the south-east of *I-124* has a multitude of fish but no sea snakes. The large gropers are not "man-eating" although this was often thought to be true prior to a more environmentally-friendly approach to diving – they do have a defence mechanism of opening their immense mouth towards a threat, which often makes a diver think of impending doom or the Sydney Harbour tunnel... *I-124* never carried deck-mounted

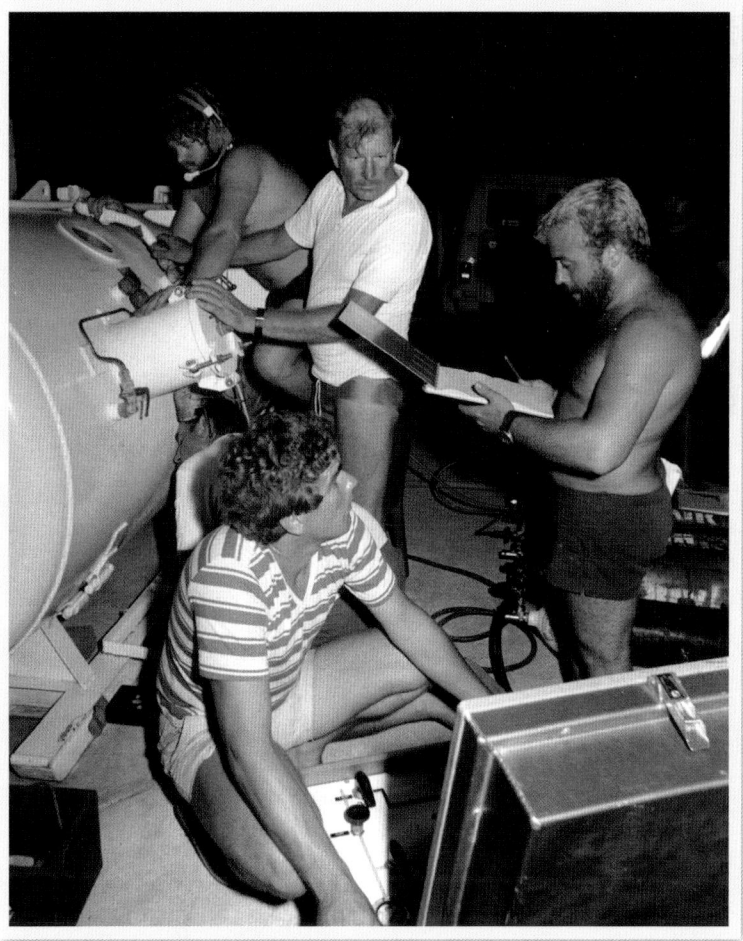

Harry Baxter (centre) tending his recompression chamber. On the intercom to a nurse inside the chamber is Harry McSherry. Noting details on a clipboard is well-known NT commercial diver Tim Proctor, while Joe Steinhouse operates a control panel at front. (Northern Territory News)

George Tyers (right) on a pontoon over the Japanese freighter wreck he located off the north coast of Rabaul, Papua New Guinea. The diver on the left is Tim Blake, who died tragically in a diving accident in Simpson harbour. (George Tyers)

machine guns, and finally many divers have confirmed *I-124*'s torpedo tube bow caps are closed.

Soon after, preliminary diving ownership disputes with Baxter arose, which gained considerable media coverage. According to Chadderton's report, Baxter was sent to Melbourne to negotiate finance for salvage. Advertisements were placed in Australian and overseas newspapers. However, when some interest was expressed, Baxter went into business by himself. He soon returned to Darwin, but his report to Chadderton and Hawks, that there had been little response to his attempts to raise finance, was met with suspicion after a few days, when according to his partners, he began spending money on a new expensive car and various other possessions. Some days later Chadderton reports he saw Henri Bource, a well known underwater photographer, down at Baxter's boat while a big decompression chamber was being loaded aboard. Both of these incidents were enough to rouse Baxter's partners' suspicions.

After some investigations Chadderton and Hawks say they found that Baxter had entered an agreement for $110,000 with a southern financier, a Mr Jim Nason[4] - an arrangement Mr Nason later confirmed in an interview. Baxter had brought with him, according to Chadderton's report: "a film crew and professional divers from Sub-Sea Services". On this news, it seems that Chadderton and Hawks decided to stay moored over the *I-124* site. Eventually Sub-Sea Services, together with Baxter and Nason, and probably accompanied by others such as Henri Bource and a diver named Gene Ainsworth of "Ocean Systems", went to sea and soon arrived at the site. After some heated discussion Chadderton and Hawks agreed to let the newcomers dive; however, they denied the validity of any contract Baxter may have taken out. At the time, as may be expected, Hawks and Chadderton were themselves planning their own version of salvage and had been writing to the Department of Foreign Affairs, engaging lawyers McCormack and Company to act for them.

Sub-Sea Services proceeded to dive for Baxter. Their report, dated "8th March, 1973", was made after four descents, and signed by a PJ Washington, Managing Director. Interesting points include:

- Dive 1. "Depth 160'. Visibility 30' +. Net cutter is 5' high. Starboard side elevators are O.K. Hatch is at an angle of 25° and Cannon is apt (sic) of hatch but forrard of conning tower. There are two holes, one in the bow and one man made."

- Dive 2. "...two open hatches, one has a door, the other has not. There is no visible damage to Port side Bow and no damage around gun emplacement. There is an open hatch on port side near gun emplacement, and blown hatch apt (sic) of conning tower and minor damage to hatchway. On port side, behind gun, grating is missing from deck. Forward of conning tower is an open hole. Port side of conning tower is a bad hole. Port and starboard lights are intact. 40' astern of conning tower on port side is an open hatch badly overgrown..." Dive 3 was aborted.

- Dive 4. "Found mortor (sic) bomb at conning tower. Vessel has list of approximately 30° to starboard. Under side of hull is exposed from rear of well forrard past propeller shafts. Propellers are intact. Apt (sic) of conning tower is rack of depth charges or mines... There is no visible damage to hull other than a hole in conning tower and open hatches. All open hatches have the dogs opened on them with the exception of the stern hatch, which appears to be twisted from an explosion....My opinion is that the vessel can be salvaged intact but the operation would require a well equipped barge with several compressors...We do not know for sure whether the torpedo tubes are open or closed...."[a]

---

a   The mention of the "mortor bomb" is interesting. Perhaps this was the small bomb – unexploded – which was dropped by the aircraft in the *I-124* action. Or it could be an unexploded shell from the submarine's deck gun.

Chadderton's report then explains what followed. Nason, he says:

> ...indicated he would pull out as he had already been led up the garden path and
> could see trouble brewing, as we wouldn't associate with Baxter any more and he
> was tied to Baxter by contract.

After splitting into two companies the potential salvors began contesting the site. According to Chadderton, Baxter formed a company called Salvage Unlimited with various individuals. Chadderton's report states that these people bought a "local landing craft and from time to time made armed raids on my tug moored to the submarine" – shots may have been fired in an attempt at intimidation is suggested in interviews with Chadderton, Hawks and others. Some more detail is provided by papers from Garrick Gray & Company, Barristers and Solicitors, which detail that a company called "T. & L. Salvage of the New Hebrides" had entered into a contract with Harry Baxter. The papers set out Baxter's attempts to sell film rights for $100, 000 and a preparation to enter into "a firm contract for the sale of the submarine to the Japanese Government for $A2.5 million where she lies..."

At this time Hawks and Chadderton were loosely joined by a local diver, George Tyers, who made a number of dives onto the wreck. He remembers on one dive he descended to the bow, at a depth of about 130 feet, and then swam back along the starboard side of the hull, which was largely clear of the sand below. Just before the conning tower he swam under the hull to the port side and then ascended. The submarine, Tyers thinks, is quite buoyant, meaning that many compartments could still be withstanding the outside sea. (Warships are divided up into watertight compartments, to prevent fire and flood damage spreading – I-124 would have been closed up for depthcharging when sunk.) He reported on a small hole in the conning tower and was of the opinion that the pressure hull beneath it had in no way been breached.

The consortium was considering possibilities of salvage at this stage, and Tyers is mentioned in one of McCormack and Company's letters as being of the opinion that if his team "...float the submarine with compressed air, it could be refloated at minimum cost". At the same time they retained the services of a Japanese national with Northern Territory experience – a Mr Hiroshi Amemiya, who had been for some years the technical manager of Golun-Kyokyuo Fishing, a company which had based several trawlers in Darwin. Mr Amemiya was asked to make direct representation to the Japanese government, which he duly did, also having some contact with the "daughter of the late captain". Hawks recalls these contacts were numerous, with some "40 letters from her" through the lawyers retained by himself and Chadderton.

An ex-IJN Navy veteran, Mr Amemiya also made investigations into the submarine's hull construction and possibilities for raising using a shipborne crane, but found that the Japanese

Fusae Kishigami – the wife of I-124's captain – prays at a family shrine with her grandson Kazuo beside her. The salvage controversy stirred up bitter feelings in Japan. (Atsuko Kishigami)

salvage authorities were not impressed with the economics of salvaging the wreck for scrap, mainly because of the depth involved. Hiroshi Amemiya also confirmed that the "Japanese government has already conducted a survey to salvage *I-124* in 1956." This was probably the genesis of the sea trip taken by Fujita Salvage to assess the site before they left after salvaging the harbour wrecks.

The Hawks/Chadderton consortium seemed to be progressing well. McCormack and Company reported their proposals were receiving serious consideration in Japan, and that Baxter was on the outer: "They look on Baxter as a pirate and he has no chance of any sort of obtaining salvage rights". Then Hawks and Chadderton left the site permanently, to show their good faith, and continued negotiations. The sea over *I-124* was quickly taken over by Baxter, who anchored over the submarine in his boat.

The salvage attempts meanwhile were receiving considerable media attention, which reached Japan. In March 1973 the Japanese Government wrote to Baxter through T&L Salvage, warning

A blurred photo of financier Jim Nason with what was to be the only spoils for the 1970s salvage teams – the diving klaxon from the I-124. (Sid Hawks)

that "all necessary steps" would be taken to prevent salvage. The diver was reported in the Japanese press as threatening to "blow up" the submarine to prevent this: "If they try to get it up they can have it – in little pieces", one paper reported, and Baxter was reported as saying that "explosive charges" had been placed on the submarine. Baxter also reported to the paper that *I-124* contained "about 80 skeletons in the perfectly preserved ship" and "mercury worth about $500, 000", although the Japanese government denied this latter claim. Baxter also said that an armed guard was "at the site 24 hours a day".

The Japanese government quickly accused Baxter of being "very inhumane" and complained that the Australian government had refused to give assurance the salvage would be stopped. The Australian government, however, was indeed doing something – it had referred the matter to the Attorney-General's Department – and on March 25 sent a Navy patrol boat, *HMAS Advance*, to the wreck site, with a "request" that any possible salvage attempts be stopped until ownership was decided. Baxter agreed to return to Darwin, although he suggested in a 1995 interview that he was somewhat coerced, saying he was arrested by the government security organisation ASIO at this point. ASIO, when asked about this, said they have never had any power to arrest anyone, and if they had wanted to talk to Baxter then a police force would have been involved. However, the NT Police confirm they have never arrested Baxter, as did the Australian Federal Police, although they said they had "had some talks". Jim Nason, the Melbourne financier, also by now seems to have completely pulled out of Baxter's plans, and he concedes that he was: "not quite conned, but almost".

Meanwhile Johnny Chadderton, Sid Hawks and George Tyers had been negotiating with Japanese authorities for salvage. They were initially pleased to see the Navy's involvement, although subsequently seemed to have become discouraged, and eventually dropped ideas of salvage. Feelings against Baxter were bitter – it is noteworthy that Chadderton's report, written for an unknown readership, dates from after Harry Baxter's next attempt at salvage, and concludes by stating that: "All the news cuttings stem from Baxter, who had a friend in the editor of the paper". Interviews with Hawks and Tyers suggest that if it were not for this unwelcome media coverage, salvage may have gone ahead. It is also worth noting that the group in its initial stages had indeed been searching for the submarine and made its first dives without gaining attention. If the media had not been attracted it is indeed possible, looking at the tone of the 1973 letters from Japan, that the submarine would have indeed been raised.[5]

Following some inactivity, in 1976 Harry Baxter was reported to be trying new recovery attempts. He said to the *NT News* that he was anchored on the site of the wreck and that "... every dive down to the wreck was being recorded on film". This time, the diver said, he had "caught up with my international law and there is nothing anybody can do to me in those waters". Baxter said to the *News* that his salvage attempts had penetrated the hull and: "...some of our divers have seen bodies sitting on the engines, but their heads have rolled away". He said, too, that he intended to reveal the mysteries of the boat: "... his divers had been into the captain's cabin , but had not yet brought up the safe from that cabin".

In 1995 he elaborated on these dives, stating that bones had been recovered, near the conning tower. He also described seeing "slats" on the outside of the submarine, which covered "cargo". (This probably describes the outer hull of the submarine, a system of lattice-like metal which housed items which could be exposed to the sea: mines, boats, drums and so on. This differs from the modern concept of a submarine, where everything is enclosed in the cause of streamlining and producing as little cavitation noise as possible.)

At least one "relic" from the submarine has been recovered. Baxter was reported in the *NT News* on 21 October 1976 as having "brought into the open two relics from a Japanese submarine ..." Hawks does remember seeing a klaxon from the outside of the submarine's conning tower brought to the surface, but he recalls that as being during the 1973 dives. Speaking to biographer Ruary Bucknall, he said:

> ...about five minutes they were down...they had a telephone... "can you send me down a net bag?" So we sent him down a net bag with a weight in it and he put

something in it – heavy – and we pulled it up. And without the barnacles being knocked off I could see it was a klaxon – a bronze klaxon – and there were marks on it where a wire rope had slithered down alongside it and shore three bolts off.

The klaxon, he thinks, was taken to Melbourne, and later seized by the Federal Police. However, in 1995, an inspection of the complete Federal Police file on *I-124* did not show anything relating to a "klaxon" or similar object. Nor did the NT Police have any record of ever having seized such an object. In fact, the klaxon was retained by financier Jim Nason, who still has it today – the sole reward for his monetary input, which he estimated at around about $100, 000.00.[b]

Baxter also claimed in a 1995 interview to have entered the submarine's forward torpedo room. "The net cutter is above this, and the torpedo room itself is flooded, with torpedoes in racks inside. The bulkhead door into the rest of the submarine is shut". This is also where "a couple of skulls" had been recovered, but they "turned to chalk in the air" and disintegrated. However, it might be noted that Baxter's entry claim is in conflict with the design of many torpedo tubes, which were designed with an interlock to make it mechanically impossible to have both ends open at any one time – a feature significantly present on many German submarines of the World War I and II periods.

It might further be noted that a wreck penetration of this sort would be extremely difficult. At a depth of 160 feet, in low light and murky conditions, an investigating diver would need to divest himself of scuba tank, climb inside a narrow tube which was overgrown with marine life, thus restricting passage, crawl dragging the scuba tank down a tunnel of about 20 foot in length, to open the inner hatch.... Ex-RN and RAN submariner Dave Parker remembers: "I've seen a bloke go up a tube to stow wardroom duty free grog. He had to be hauled out by the heels." Parker also queries why the torpedo tubes would be open anyway: "...no captain in his right mind would go round with his bow caps open..." He further points out that even without an interlock system, the inner bow cap, presuming Baxter could get past the outer cap, would be closed, and it would be very difficult to open it from inside the torpedo tube, there being no lock mechanism on that side of the door.

George Tyers offers further reasons for supposing that the submarine has not been penetrated. He argues that no-one has been into *I-124*: "I am 99.9% sure of it", he said in 1995, citing especially the fact that he was able to swim under the hull completely and the fact that the submarine sits quite proud of the seabed to suggest that it is not very heavy; ie: not flooded. He

b   Submariner David Parker points out that the klaxon was more likely to have been on the **inside** of the conning tower: "... why on the outside? Surely not to communicate with the sharks. I can understand it being on the inside of the tower with a couple more, one in each compartment. As you may remember I told you I ended up as a P.O.E (Petty Officer Electrician) and it was our job to maintain these klaxons." This suggests that a diver may have searched around inside the top of the conning tower fairing, and forcibly removed the klaxon.

also points out that there would be a very high pressure inside from the high pressure air (used to push water out of the sub's ballast tanks and therefore ascend), plus acids, salt water, gases, diesel and so on. The whole combination would be sufficient to make any airtight space highly dangerous, and he estimated that large sections of the submarine were still watertight – and un-entered.

Meanwhile Baxter's renewed attempts were arousing the ire of the Federal Government. Local Senator Bernie Kilgariff was contacted by the then acting Minister for Foreign Affairs, Ian Sinclair, and asked to use his influence to stop Baxter. Senator Kilgariff remembers that there were "souvenirs being rumoured for sale around town; stories about divers taking items off". RSL President "Lofty" Plane remembers Baxter giving "perhaps a small bell or compass" to the RSL; the item, he thinks, may have been recovered by police shortly afterwards during a visit to the club. Again, however, there is some confusion about this: the-then head of the NT Police Special Branch, Barry Tiernan, does not remember any such items being recovered by the force, although he does recall the rumours and says it might have been possible.

Senator Bernie Kilgariff says that he felt then and still feels now that *I-124* "...was a tomb and should be regarded as such". Comparisons were drawn in Parliament between *I-124* and the Australian cruiser *HMAS Perth*, sunk near Java. "We don't want the wreck of the *Perth* and the remains of its crew interfered with," Mr Sinclair said. "You may be assured that the Government will be active in trying, by whatever means, to bring about a situation where the Japanese submarine is left undisturbed. We are in consultation with the Japanese Government..."

Meanwhile, the ongoing dispute and its ensuing publicity was forcing the hand of the Federal Government, which reacted swiftly this time to further publicity about the submarine. In 1976

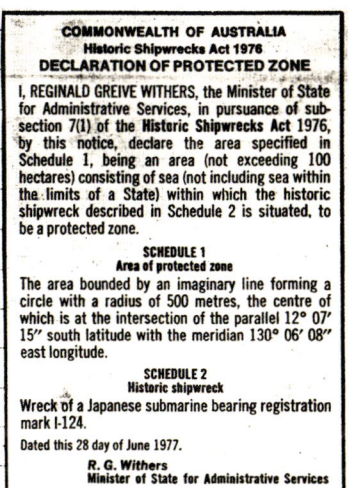

Advertisements taken out in Australian newspapers in July 1977, declaring the I-124 as a protected historic shipwreck. (Ian Gibson)

the Historic Shipwrecks Act was introduced and debated in Parliament, with some significant comments being made in the Senate. Senator Kilgariff (NT) said on 1 December 1976:

> The only reasons for entering this Japanese submarine, which I suggest ought to be looked upon as a war grave, are sensation and plundering....Having heard that entry may have been gained to the submarine - and there has been suggestion that one or two articles or gear may have been taken off it – the Japanese are very distressed that this should happen.

He went on to read a statement from Mr Ian Sinclair, then the Acting Minister for Foreign Affairs, issued when: "I endeavoured to initiate some action a few weeks ago to ensure that a person in Darwin who had been endeavouring to enter the submarine should desist." He quoted from Mr Sinclair's statement:

> The Australian Government shares the view of the Japanese Government that the submarine and the remains of its crew should be regarded as a war grave, and that it should be left to lie in peace....Australians can sympathise with the feelings of the Japanese people for the protection of the remains of their servicemen. Indeed, Australians would react in a similar way if any attempts were made to disturb, for example, the wreck of *HMAS Perth* lying in the Sunda Strait near Java, and the remains of its Australian crew.

The proposed Act however, was not sufficient to stop Baxter. The disgruntled diver attempted to destroy the wreck. Quietly, he obtained a quantity of explosives, and according to his own account in later interviews and also in comments to the media, lowered the explosives to the conning tower of the wreck, and then detonated them. He says he used plastic explosive for this: "200 pounds or four cases". However, the attempt seems to have inflicted little damage: according to later accounts from the Royal Australian Navy, the fairing around the conning tower has been detached, but otherwise the explosives failed to damage the wreck. This is not surprising: Baxter's quantity of explosive may be estimated from his own account to be less than 50 kilograms in weight, whereas the depth charges used in *Deloraine*'s attack were a quarter of an Imperial ton each and even these were not effective unless detonated extremely close to the enemy's hull.

Baxter was to talk further on his aborted salvage over the coming years. In an article in the magazine *Australasian Post*, he said that:

> A Japanese Ambassador from Washington flew out to see me, and all he seemed to be really worried about was the ship's safe. I have never seen anyone more agitated than that man, as he kept asking me over and over again: "Where is the safe? What have you done with the safe?" But I wouldn't answer that one. What I have done with the safe is my business.

In 1984, in an article in the southern *Sunday Press*, Baxter said he "blew holes in the hull." He suggested that "loot" and "secret documents" could be easily found.

> Just swim through the conning tower into the attack room. There is a door leading to the commander's cabin, a small room about three by three metres. In there is the safe....There are a lot of things in the safe, things I could not talk about at this stage.

Another possibility that may have motivated Baxter is a persistent story that Commander Kishigami's sword was a primary item for recovery: in the 1995 interviews he persisted with the claim that it was worth "a million dollars...to the captain's daughter", although he seemed vague about the origins of the tale. (Atsuko Kishigami was politely amused by this story when it was put to her.)

Baxter also claimed in the 1984 article that he had been interviewed many times by "officials" from America, Japan and Australia, who: "...want to know all I know about the contents of the safe. They're not interested in the bodies or the loot, they want to know what I know about the secret documents".

These stories raised further attention in Japan. Reports in the *Mainichi* newspaper said that "local people" were trying to "raise the submarine and scrap it". Baxter's comments on human remains also made the paper, and perhaps he suggested earlier that he had attempted to use explosives on the submarine: the *Sankei* newspaper reported in July 1977 that "the salvage company...has blasted the command tower", but also seemed optimistic that the Historic Shipwrecks Act would protect the submarine from further damage. During June 1977 papers around Australia carried notices publicising the Historic Shipwrecks Act, and it seems that Baxter then left the submarine alone.[6]

An interesting addition to the story of potential salvage is the fact that discussions took place between Johnny Chadderton[7], a Mr David Wright and Perth-based Barristers and Solicitors Cocks Macnish and Co in late 1983. These discussions centred on the intent of the statutes protecting *I-124*. The discussions concluded by determining that illegal salvage would be dangerous, that: "It is evident that there are serious consequences if you work on or take possession of the wreck".

I-124 was left once more to the multitude of fish which have made it their home. More controversy was to surround her, however: a visit from even more hopeful salvors, and a controversy over another aspect of what lies inside the wreck.

(Endnotes)

1   This description is drawn from a combination of conversations with Sid Hawks and a biography of him by Ruary Bucknall.

2   There are considerable geographical discrepancies in WWII accounts of the *I-124*'s position and the preceding actions. These are largely due to the limited navigational equipment of the time and the fact that land was not in sight for much of the proceedings, making position-fixing difficult, especially in the middle of an action.

3   *Australian Sea Heritage* magazine editor Graeme Andrews advises that *Arnhem T* was once a Navy vessel, *HMAS Warreen*.

4   Found in the "Nason Papers" file of the NT Museum is a contract which was drawn up with the following personnel, some of whom are unknown: Baxter and Lowry - 38%; Reardon and Murray - 27%; Harper and Gray - 5% each and Nason 25%.

5   Hawks died in 2004, and Hawks Court, in the NT's Acacia Hills, is named after him. The Naming of Place listing in the NT's place names register reads: "Hawks Court is named in commemoration of Sid Hawks (1907-2004) RAAF Sergeant during WWII, Hotel and Store owner; Proprietor of coastal shipping business; involved in evacuation of refugees from Timor during civil war in 1975." http://www.nt.gov.au/placenames/register/2007/documents/JarvisRdHawksCt-Herbert.pdf 14 September 2010.

6   Baxter died in the Royal Darwin Hospital, probably in the late years of the 1990s – the author's memory is unclear.

7   Johnny Chadderton maintains that the *I-124* carries valuables such as jewels and gold, looted from South-East Asia by the advancing Japanese. He suggests they would have taken advantage of any warship eventually returning to Japan to get their profits home.

CHAPTER 13

– A SERIES OF VISITORS

In 1984, after lying undisturbed for some years, *I-124* again received both visitors and controversy. Divers attempted to descend to the submarine from a private vessel, and an official dive was made to the submarine by the Royal Australian Navy. Following this, the West Australian Maritime Museum began research and visits.

The attempts to salvage *I-124* in the 1970s had obviously left their mark on Johnny Chadderton. (It will be recalled that he was one of the original team who attempted recovery of the vessel along with Sid Hawks and Harry Baxter, and he was discussing recovery with lawyers in 1983.) On 11 January, 1984, Chadderton and several other men were intercepted near the site of the wreck on board the *MV Leisure*, a small fishing boat.

Dive gear found onboard the MV Leisure by the Australian Federal Police. (Australian Federal Police)

The Fremantle patrol boat HMAS Cessnock. She had only been in service for a year when she halted the diving activities of MV Leisure at the I-124 wreck site. (Royal Australian Navy)

The interception was made by three Federal Police officers with the assistance of the Navy patrol boat *HMAS Cessnock*. The AFP, acting on information received, had been keeping the *Leisure* under surveillance for some days. Once on board, the police officers spoke to a Marcus Axton and Johnny Chadderton, who readily admitted he was the organiser of the expedition. The crew agreed to accompany the police back to Darwin.

The *MV Leisure* was duly brought back to the Darwin patrol boat base, where it was moored outboard and alongside the Navy boat. The following morning saw a front page headline about the incident in the *NT News*, accompanied by photographs. The *News* featured the "boat's skipper", Axton, pictured talking to police. He was quoted in the newspaper as saying that his vessel:

> ...had not been apprehended by the Federal Police. He said he and his crew had
> been working on a joint operation with the Navy....(*But, the same article continued*)
> The Navy has strongly denied any joint operation with the vessel.

Another interesting suggestion in the *NT News* article also proposed another "*I-124* myth": "There have been suggestions some prisoners of war were also aboard." An examination of the Federal Police files reveals the true story of the *Leisure* – a little less glamourous than these exciting suggestions.

On board the *Leisure*, according to the AFP file, were seven men: Marcus Axton – the boat's captain; John Chadderton, David Wright, Peter Henry, Allan Miller, David Barnett, and John Baylis. The *Leisure*'s crew were questioned by the Federal Police, and this revealed a number of items of interest. The expedition had, the men said, been organised to make a film about the submarine. Camera equipment had been located on board – this was to have been operated by David Barnett. Peter Henry and Allan Miller were divers, and John Baylis a deckhand. David Wright had been organising the expedition along with Chadderton.

The *Leisure*'s search had not been successful. Upon reaching the position of the submarine, the anchor had been dropped. However, soundings had not revealed anything of interest. When an attempt was made to raise the anchor, however, it was found to be snagged. Chadderton and Barnett, believing the anchor was hooked on the submarine, dived but did not locate the wreck. The boat was moved and further dives were unsuccessfully undertaken; the venture being halted by the arrival of *HMAS Cessnock*. All of the men stated that they were unaware of any law concerning the submarine.

The *Leisure* had been quite close to finding *I-124*: the Federal Police later sought the assistance of Lieutenant Peter Collett, the Assistant Operations Officer at the Darwin Naval Headquarters. Lieutenant Collett marked on charts for the AFP the position of the *Leisure* and the gazetted prohibited zone of *I-124*; the fishing boat had been just outside the circle to the northwest.

The Australian Government Solicitor, acting on the advice of a former Crown Prosecutor, was subsequently of the opinion:

> ...the Prosecution would be unlikely to establish a prima facie case against any of the group members for any offence under the Crimes Act 1914...Counsel does not consider that there is sufficient evidence of an agreement to effect an unlawful purpose or of an attempt to commit any offence.

In the event the file on the *MV Leisure* was closed. Johnny Chadderton, however, was obviously a person who liked a varied and exciting life, for in 1986 he was again in a sea controversy, this time being in much colder waters. Operating near the French dependency islands of Amsterdam and St. Paul, and on board the 59 metre Australian trawler *Southern Raider*, skipper Chadderton and a crew of 22 were chased and fired upon by the French patrol boat *Albatros*. The patrol boat eventually sank the fishing vessel, then picked up the crew, who were placed under arrest and taken to Reunion Island. Having been held there for some time Chadderton says he and a crewmember – Alistair Annandale – windsurfed some considerable distance to Mauritius Island in an effort to escape. The story, once analysed, is a confused tangle of drug allegations, fishing ground incursions, possible bomb test sites and even simply a mistaken identity. Chadderton and the crew were eventually released and an apology was later made by the French government.

Some time after the *Leisure* incident, in 1984 stories about the presence of mines on the deck

The Ton-class minesweeper HMAS Curlew, which entered RAN service in 1962 after having already served for almost a decade in the Royal Navy as HMS Chediston. A dive team from Curlew dived on I-124 in 1984. (Royal Australian Navy)

of the submarine began to circulate in the NT community. An unverified story claimed that a mine had come loose from the submarine and had been destroyed, "according to a Navy signal, by rifle fire". The source of these stories is difficult to determine – suggestions have been made it was Harry Baxter. It then seems the NT Government made representation to the Navy, and asked if the safety of *I-124*'s war stores could be determined. In due course, a dive team was despatched on board *HMAS Curlew*, a Ton class minesweeper, to investigate the submarine and determine the safety of any ordnance carried. The dives were carried out quietly, and nothing of the descents or their consequences was reported by the media.

The dives were the most professional ever made, and are fascinating in their accuracy. A preliminary dive was carried out on 5 November 1984, and confirmed the presence of the submarine. The following morning descents began, using paired divers breathing a nitrox mix.[1] The forward section of the submarine was inspected first and the following day the stern section, with the underside of the wreck and surrounding seabed being the final areas surveyed.

Lieutenant Commander Russ Crane, who led the team (when this book was first published a Captain in the RAN; then by this edition the Chief of the Navy), made a detailed report of the dives. Two sections of Lieutenant Commander's Crane's report are of especial interest:

> The hull lies stem to stern, North to South in approximately 45 metres of water. Mine carrying rails are visible from the stern to the protrusions aft of the conning tower. Two of these protrusions are clearly hatches, one shut and one fully open.

> The after section of the Conning Tower for a distance of about one metre has been torn from the main Conning Tower structure and is now littered across the

deck on the starboard side....An estimated 75% of the structure remains upright with aerials intact. The Direction Finding Aerial is clearly visible...Forward of the Conning Tower to the bow no extraneous objects are visible apart from the 5.5 inch gun. This appeared to be in excellent condition with the barrel level.

According to Crane's later recollections, visibility was generally around four to five metres. "Things were generally shut and closed down. We found no openings into the submarine. The torpedo tubes at the bow were all closed." Using five Clearance Divers plus himself on the descents, Crane also confirmed the submarine: "... is sitting on its keel and seems remarkably well preserved for the time spent on the bottom..." and is: "quite proud of the seabed", which may well indicate – as said before – that most of the casing is watertight. Some indentations in the casing were found, but it was hard to determine whether this damage was due to Baxter's explosives or to WWII damage. Crane also reported in a later interview that: "...there were no obvious signs of entry however I could not rule out the possibility...."

Harry Baxter had claimed that 41 mines were still on the submarine, a suggestion that must be inaccurate, given she released 27 mines in January 1942. However, it certainly may be the case that some mines are still in their racks inside the submarine's aft mine room. Lieutenant Commander Crane had been briefed on the submarine's construction, although he says the divers were not aware of the details of the aft mine release gear, and he confirms that the team knew of *I-124*'s hull construction and capacity for outside storage. As well as checking the mine carrying rails the divers made a detailed search between the inner and outer hulls of the submarine. No mines were found.

How did the dive team feel about their exploration of such a significant and mysterious wreck? Crane reported: "...the general feeling of the team during the dives was one of respect for the men of *I-124* and recognition of the rights of these men to remain ...free of the pilferers of wartime wrecks."

At this point is it worth noting the discrepancies between the dive reports of the various descents onto the wreck that may well have led to the mine confusion in the first place. It will be recalled that the 1942 divers reported: "a V shaped well at forward part and abreast conning tower about 15 to 20 foot long and 6 feet inside. Apparently peace time boat stowage". Chadderton's report said that: "The aft deck has 2 rows of petrol drums in brackets, which are intact..." Sub-Sea Services also reported: "Dive 4. Found mortor (sic) bomb at conning tower.... Apt (sic) of conning tower is rack of depth charges or mines...." The RAN team's report, made by expert divers over a longer period, does not report such objects. Why is this so?

The variety of different reports about the shape of *I-124*'s hull is due to the very nature of the

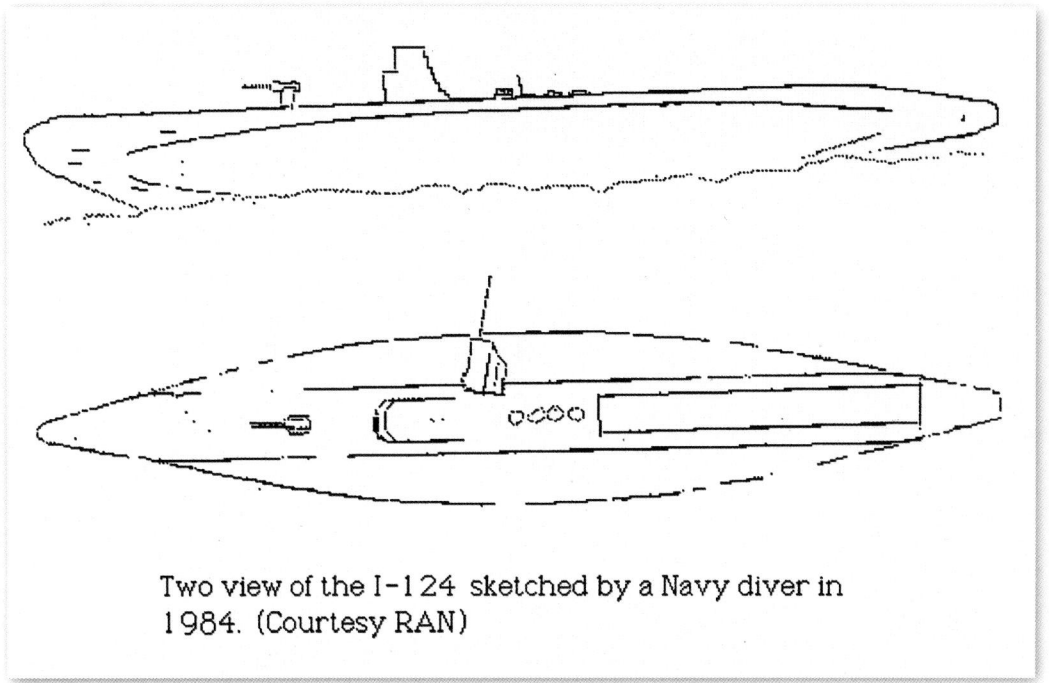

Two view of the I-124 sketched by a Navy diver in 1984. (Courtesy RAN)

Two views of the I-124 sketched by RAN divers from the Curlew dives. (Royal Australian Navy)

boat's construction. The boats of WWII were in general possessed of a "double" hull. Inside is a pressure hull, an immensely strong container that resists the enormous pressures of the sea outside, and provides a life-supporting environment for the submariners. The outer or surrounding hull is technically known as a "free flooding outer hull", and is open to the sea. Part of this design allows the inward flow of sea water, which is flooded into ballast tanks, thus making the submarine sink. The nature of this type of hull also had the added virtue of allowing the storage of various items which are not harmed by seawater. In addition, some designers preferred this sort of hull as it would make the submarine much harder to damage: any torpedo or depth charge impact would be taken on the outer hull, with the inner area of water cushioning the shock.[2]

In the dim light of the depths, with vision obscured by growth, poor visibility and tiny fish, divers can easily make assumptions and mistakes. (It should also be remembered that *I-124* lies at a depth where nitrogen narcosis is a possibility.) What might the divers have seen and converted into various items? Perhaps the Sub-Sea Services divers and Johnny Chadderton saw torpedo containers, ballast tanks or other parts of the hull, and mistook these for mines. Alternatively perhaps, there were mines contained between the two hulls and they did escape – perhaps loosened from their long captivity by Harry Baxter's explosives. Whatever the case, it would seem that the Navy's inspection has laid to rest the idea that there are any "loose mines" attached to *I-124*.

In an interesting postscript, in 1988, three ships of the Japanese Navy, by then known as the Japanese Maritime Self-Defence Force, visited Darwin as part of a goodwill cruise to Papua New Guinea and Australia. The Hatsuyuki class destroyers *Shimayuki* (DD133), *Setoyuki* (DD131), and the Training Ship *Katori* (TV3501) were in Darwin's port for a short time. A wreath was laid at sea and commemorative rifle volleys were fired, and the ship's embarked musicians played a small concert in Darwin Central Business District's Raintree Park to commemorate the sunken submarine. In later years other Japanese ships have marked their visit by various ceremonies.

In early 1989, the Western Australian Maritime Museum began preparations to send a research team north to investigate several shipwrecks sites. One of these was possibly the *SS Koombana*, lost around 20 March, 1912, somewhere off Port Hedland. A possible wreck site had been found for the vessel by a David Tomlinson, master of the research vessel *Flamingo Bay*, based in Darwin. Following considerable evidence of something in the area, the Museum decided to investigate in their capacity as the delegate of the Federal Minister responsible for the Department of The Arts, Sport, the Environment, Territories and Tourism (DASETT).

The WA Maritime Museum was also interested in the wreck of an iron barque, the *Ann Millicent*, and the planned expedition received some sponsorship from the NT Museum to investigate this too. The wreck of *I-124* was suggested for investigation. This would also allow minor investigation into suggestions that mercury was leaking into the sea from the wreck and resulting in abnormally high levels of the chemical in the local goldband snapper. Some of the other curiosities about *I-124* could also be resolved, according to David Tomlinson – he pointed out the multiple contacts in the WWII reports, and also highlighted claims made by a person who said he had dived on "a submarine" which was fitted with a German compass on the bridge, and an aeroplane hangar but without a gun. Added to these mysteries were Hiroyuki Agawa's claims that the submarine was in shallow water and had been entered, and Polmar and Carpenter's supporting evidence.

Japanese officers and sailors commemorate the sinking of I-124 over the site during a three-ship visit to Darwin in 1988. (Japanese Maritime Self-Defence Force)

Flamingo Bay during her I-124 investigation. (WA Maritime Museum)

The well-equipped *Flamingo Bay* was the vessel chosen for the enterprise, and it was planned to embark a team made up of NT and WA Museum personnel, as well as a Port Hedland-based group who had been searching for the *Koombana*. The Western Australia team was led by Mike McCarthy, from the Department of Maritime Archaeology of the Western Australian Maritime Museum, who later produced an extremely comprehensive report on the voyage. *I-124*, which was off-limits as a war grave, was approved for this special occasion as a dive site by the Federal Government.

Once in Darwin, however, all did not go smoothly. The weather was very bad, and for several days the *Flamingo Bay* expedition sat in port, its crew taking the opportunity to accumulate stores, test equipment, and talk to people about the submarine, including local historian Peter Dermoudy, who retained a long interest in *I-124*. The NT team eventually withdrew, after, according to the report of WA Maritime Museum leader McCarthy: "...highly political developments". These basically were twofold: as McCarthy says: "...the Japanese government had apparently expressed concern on the basis of the fears that divers would disturb the human remains on board" and "...the Northern Territory Government was, at the time, apparently undertaking a feasibility study on the possibility of raising the vessel for display purposes". The latter was indeed true, as will be enlarged upon in a later chapter. David Tomlinson finds this "mystifying....we had offered to make two cabins available for Japanese guests, so that they could ensure we were doing the right thing....we were not going out as a pirate!" Despite the signing of an undertaking before the Australian Federal Police that the team would not dive on *I-124*, the NT team was pulled out the day before departure, and this was followed by a withdrawal by NT Museum Director Colin Jack-Hinton (in his capacity as the Federal Government's representative) of the special licence originally given to dive.

The expedition left port anyway, visited the *I-124* wreck, the *Ann Millicent* site, and then the supposed location of the *Koombana*, where unfortunately only an abandoned oil rig was found.

Although the primary mission of the *Flamingo Bay* voyage was unfulfilled, the expedition did make a valuable contribution towards understanding the history of *I-124* and its present state. The ship arrived at the wreck site at 4am on 16 March 1989. Side scan sonar was deployed, with the ship remaining outside the "off-limits" zone. When nothing was found, the search area was widened, and at around 9am that day, *I-124* was located with a north/south attitude towards the south some 500 metres **outside** the zone.

Having anchored, in a remarkable display of fortitude, the expedition held to the spirit of the Historic Shipwrecks Act, and did not send down their embarked divers, deploying a Remote Operated Vehicle (ROV) instead, supplied by Underwater Systems Australia. This machine, "flown" over the wreck with considerable skill by a Mr Graham Thompson, transmitted pictures of the wreck to the surface, where they were viewed on television monitors. The ROV landed, (according to a later report by Jon Carpenter, the on-board WA Maritime Museum specialised on-site conservator), on the: "bow area of the submarine, from here it traveled along the foredeck towards the conning tower". The pictures showed periscope tubes without the shroud of the outer conning tower, perhaps detached by Harry Baxter's explosives:

> the conning tower appeared to have lost all the metal fairings, which would have streamlined the structure, leaving three prominent protrusions sticking up. This may have been the remains of periscope etc. The direction finding radar[3] ring was clearly visible and intact.

The Remote Operated Vehicle is prepared for a "flight" over the wreck. (WA Maritime Museum)

MV Larrapan, workboat of Sid Hawks, later bought by Johnny Chadderton. (Sid Hawks)

The gun was visible too, but a more detailed inspection was denied to the expedition due to the strong tides, and various technical problems – six out of the eight ROV deployments were not given their full operational time due to problems. The *Flamingo Bay* had press personnel embarked, and the ROV footage was used in TV news items. However, that was the extent of the inspection, even when the ROV cable became entangled in the down line to the wreck and divers had to be deployed to free it. They descended to about 100 feet for this purpose, only some 50 feet above the wreck, but did not go any deeper, again adding to the sense of frustration on board, which was probably occasionally irritated further by the occasional overflight by Coastwatch aircraft, as McCarthy notes in his diary.

The following day searches were made for any second submarine perhaps sunk nearby, but despite initial excitement at a possible find, nothing was discovered. Further research established that the German compass story originated from the manager of the 1970s diving company Sub-Sea Services, and its accuracy was in doubt. The *Flamingo Bay* and its expedition departed for its next research site, having experienced some disappointments, but having performed a useful service and obtained some interesting video footage.

The position of the submarine site has subsequently been corrected, and the zone now encompasses *I-124*. It is worth noting that the original survey had been performed prior to the invention of the highly accurate Global Positioning System.

(Endnotes)

1   Master SCUBA instructor Sasha Muller advises that this refers to breathing a mixture of air with the oxygen component boosted to allow greater endurance at depth. Neon has also been used as a breathing medium, which appears to be completely free of narcotic effects. Another breathing gas utilised is "trimix", made up of oxygen and two dilutant gases (usually nitrogen and helium). Closed Circuit Rebreathers are also now being introduced into the world of sport-diving (previously being confined to military use) and these too will allow much more freedom at depth; a luxury the WWII, 1970's and 1980's divers on *I-124* did not enjoy.

2   The USSR-designed Foxtrot submarine utilises this philosophy; however the damage-limitation design of the free-flooding outer hull also makes this type of boat particularly noisy in sonar terms.

3   Actually the **radio** direction finding antenna.

MV Leisure tied up alongside HMAS Cessnock in the Royal Australian Navy's patrol boat base, Darwin. (Australian Federal Police)

An underwater photo of an open hatch on the I-124 wreck. For some years there were persistent fears of mercury leaking into surrounding waters. (Royal Australian Navy)

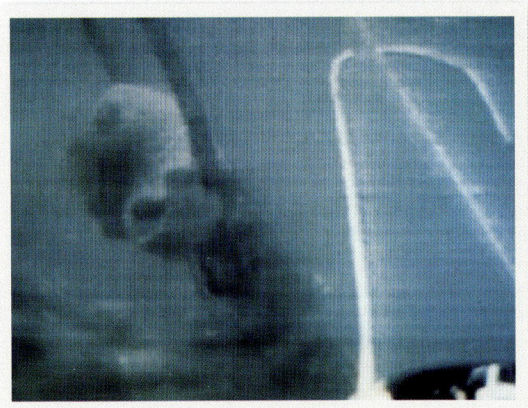

The radio DF (Direction Finding) loop, again as seen by the ROV. (WA Maritime Museum)

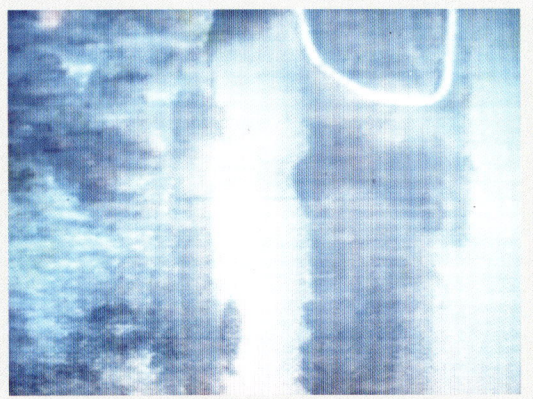

The periscope standards of I-124, as seen from a Remote Operated Vehicle (ROV) operated from the RV Flamingo Bay, in 1989, while the ship was carrying out a search operation for the West Australian Maritime Museum. (WA Maritime Museum)

CHAPTER 14

– MERCURY AND A PROPOSAL TO RAISE

The suggestion that the element mercury was carried on board *I-124* received considerable media attention from the 1970s salvage attempts through to the 1990s. Questions were asked in the Senate as recently as in 1992, for example, inquiring as to the presence of mercury on board the wreck. On this occasion Northern Territory Senator Bob Collins was able to answer confidently and definitively. This was not always the case – in 1989 amidst the *Flamingo Bay* arguments the suggestion that mercury was on board the submarine was much in debate.

Mercury, of course, is a highly poisonous substance. Large amounts of the element leaking into the sea would inevitably find its way into fish, with disastrous consequences for the local fishing industry in Darwin. The mere suggestion that NT fish were contaminated would doubtlessly result in a sharp drop in consumption.

The suggestion that *I-124* contained mercury took three forms. First, it was suggested that mercury was carried as ballast. Second, it was theorised that mercury was carried in the cargo, and third, that instruments on board the submarine contained the chemical.

Why would a submarine carry mercury as ballast? Submarines use different types of ballast, loosely divided into two categories: that used to control the submarine's descent and ascent, and that used to maintain the submarine's equilibrium – this latter is usually known as 'trim" ballast. The first category of ballast was not what mercury was envisaged for. The diving and ascending of a submarine has always been controlled by virtually altering the buoyancy of the submarine. Large ballast tanks are filled with water, or alternatively water is displaced by air supplied from inside the submarine and carried in compressed air bottles. If these tanks are flooded with water, the submarine becomes heavier and sinks. If these ballast tanks alternatively have air forced into them the submarine becomes lighter, and rises.

However, altering the trim of the submarine is the job of another type of ballast. It can be easily understood that many things will cause a submarine at depth to have its equilibrium alter, thus causing either the bow or the stern to rise or sink. The movement of objects inside the submarine; the firing of a torpedo or the release of a mine, even people moving about – all will alter a submarine's trim. This can lead to embarrassing results: imagine if a torpedo was fired and this loss of bow weight was followed by the submarine's bow breaking the surface, thus giving away her position. As such, a submarine's trim is extremely important, so much so that in each submarine in any navy there is a crew member designated as "trimming officer" whose job it is to keep the boat precisely balanced.

The qualities of mercury might very well mean that it was a possibility for use in trimming a submarine. In trimming, something is needed that can be pumped to and fro along the length of a submarine. Mercury, being less liquid in its movement than water, might have been considered a better type of ballast than water. Indeed, some modern submarines do have a trim ballast of mercury or oil or both. The possibility that I-124's ballast was composed of mercury may very well have been researched by Baxter, but this is unlikely, as such specific peculiarities of submarine design are not widely known or easily researched. Perhaps though, the theory was once suggested, and then easily seized upon.

Where else might the mercury suggestion come from? Baxter certainly used it as a justification for salvage in the 1970s – his typed report about discovery and first dives on the submarine contains the statement: "...it is possible that the ship contains Mercury which was used for ballast which would be worth $1 million", and he at another time within that period claimed a figure of $500, 000. The Japanese Government issued a denial of this, but Baxter was not deterred, perhaps because he may have been using the amounts as bait for finance.

Stories of mercury being carried in submarines were also perhaps caused by the 1950s dives on the wreck of the German submarine U-853. Still relatively easily diveable off the United States' New England coast, this unfortunate vessel was pillaged by divers, who carried off bones, sextants, binoculars, books, pieces of the periscopes, the two bronze propellers and various other items. Henry Keatts and George Farr detail the salvage campaign thoroughly in *Dive Into History*, and note that finally after fruitless attempts during the 1950s, the most persistent and well organised of the divers, one Oswald. L. Bonifay, revealed that he was after mercury, which he believed was on board in steel flasks. Other abortive salvage attempts followed in the 60s, but nothing of the supposed mercury cargo has ever been found.

Baxter may also have been influenced at the time by the salvage of the German submarine U-859, sunk in 1944 close to Penang, an island off the Malaysian west coast. This submarine had been carrying a cargo of 70 tons of mercury when it was sunk, and in 1972 amidst worldwide publicity a salvage company began raising the chemical. Baxter undoubtedly knew of this salvage.

Mike McCarthy, of the WA Maritime Museum, while researching this theory, came across an interesting story about the German submarine which may well have been known to Baxter and fuelled his enthusiasm:

> In 1976 for example, an apparently loosely knit, Australian salvage company called "The Group" dived on the German submarine U859 which was sunk by *HMS Trenchant* in 120 feet of water about 25 miles north-west of Pinang (Penang) Island. According to Mr John Bastian, a member of the diving team, about "40 tons" of mercury were recovered from the submarine which had been cut in two by the engagement such that the two sections lay about 50 metres apart. According to Mr Bastian, who in my opinion is a very reliable source and whose comments have been supported by others, the group was aware that the submarine carried mercury and located it in small "steel flasks" not much larger than portable oxygen bottles in common use today. These were found stowed horizontally in layers in the keel, in compartments aft of the conning tower which measured around "3 feet wide by four feet deep". The compartments apparently bounded by the frames of the vessel and the keel itself. When the news of their find spread, the group were effectively dispossessed of the mercury by the West German Government. (41)

There is certainly evidence from newspaper reports at the time that a treasure-trove of mercury was one of the reasons Baxter was eager to salvage the submarine, which contained, according to an *NT News* report of the time: "...about 18 tons of mercury". And conservationists of the day – like their counterparts of the 1980s – were understandably quick to voice concern over any prospect of leaking mercury: "...the whole bloody thing sounds bloody dangerous", said one, a Mr Jack Veal; "....if anything went wrong and the mercury escaped it would ruin the whole ecology of the coastline." However, the mercury story received little attention in the 1970s, and was soon submerged in the ongoing row about the salvage of the submarine, perhaps reflecting the environmental attitudes of the time, as the re-occurrence of the story in the late 1980s received far more publicity.

In 1989 two articles suggesting that mercury was contained in *I-124* were published by a Mr David Hancock. The first was entitled "Jap Subs are still Menacing Darwin" and was contained in an April edition of *The Australian*. The same writer then had a reworked version of the article published in *People* magazine: "The Sub with a Million Secrets" (May 1989). Hancock interviewed Darryl Grey of the NT Fisheries Department about a survey of mercury in sharks. In a wide-ranging piece, the mercury report joined the stories of the trapped Japanese, the "connection" to *HMAS Sydney* and the 1970s salvage attempts in rekindling interest in *I-124*. To add to the air of mystery, Hancock included snippets such as suggestions by divers that "...there was a hangar on the front deck, no gun and net-cutting apparatus on the bow", and even a photo supposedly taken "from the deck of an Australian Navy corvette...just before *HMAS*

Details of a mine laid by the minelaying squadron and later recovered from a Northern Territory beach. This mine now has an inspection window and is on display at the RAN shore establishment, HMAS Penguin. (RAN and David Stevens)

Deloraine sank a Japanese submarine". (This photo included an aircraft, a Bristol Beaufighter, which NT aviation historian Bob Alford identifies as a model which did not appear in the Darwin area until November 1942 – and this particular aircraft also carries post-war roundels and markings....)

Soon there was debate aplenty in the NT community. Heated letters to the Editor of the local *NT News* were accompanied by equally heated letters to other papers such as *The Australian*. Other people quickly joined the argument. George Tyers, the diver who had been brought into the Hawks/Chadderton partnership, was interviewed by the local paper, and branded the mercury claims as "garbage". Meanwhile, the Australian Marine Sciences Association called upon the Federal Government to reverse its decision to ban an investigatory dive. This was refused.

The final debunking of the *I-124* mercury theory is due almost solely to the efforts of Mike McCarthy at the Western Australian Museum. He researched the proposal extensively and thoroughly, and his comprehensive report finally laid the suggestion to rest, although as has been pointed out above, the suggestion of mercury escaping from the submarine is still sometimes made.

McCarthy's investigation of the mercury possibility was made as part of the *Flamingo Bay's* voyage to the submarine site. Compiling a document entitled "*I-124*, WW2 Japanese Submarine. (Investigation into the Trim and Ballast System)", two of Mr McCarthy's assistants, a Mr Graham Thompson and a Mr A. Shaw, from British Shipbuilders Ltd, concluded that *I-124*'s German predecessor did not have a design that was capable of using mercury ballast. Further, the *U-125* class used "iron ballast and sea water as trimming ballast". McCarthy's further enquiries to the German government also found that "no German submarines had mercury trim or ballast". The Japanese government also conducted their own historical research and in a meeting with DASETT confirmed that "in the I class submarines seawater was used as trimming ballast"; Japanese submarines had carried mercury transferred from German submarines as a war material from Penang to Japan, but *I-124* was not one of these and had not visited Penang either.

It is notable that Senator Collins referred exclusively to McCarthy's report in his 1992 Senate answer.

A PROPOSAL TO RAISE *I-124*

In the late 1980s a new project to salvage the submarine was launched. This affair was a business-like proposition, managed to a large degree by a Mr Don Kibbler, who had achieved some fame in the 1970s and 1980s as the originator and driving force behind the well-known Japanese war cemetery in Cowra, NSW. Don Kibbler, living and working in the town as a newsagent, saw the famous breakout as being an essential part of Cowra's history. Although he was too young to fight in World War II, and had no particular attachment to Japan, he began a project that would take nearly 20 years. At first, Kibbler's thoughts of the nearby prisoner of war camp were dominated by his memories of "slant-eyed men behind wire", for as a boy he had stared at the many men who were imprisoned there in increasing numbers as the Allies drove the Japanese back across the Pacific to the Home Islands. In August 1943, over 1, 100 Japanese prisoners of war, desperate to make amends for their capture, broke out of the NSW camp in what for some was a suicide attempt. 231 prisoners and four Australian soldiers died; in some cases the Japanese took their own lives rather than face further disgrace in recapture: some lay down on railway lines and were decapitated.

In 1964 the cemetery where the escapees were buried was designated as the burial place for any Japanese who died on Australian soil in WWII. In 1970, Kibbler began planning the Cowra Japanese Garden. Donations to help the project flooded in, and a Japanese architect was employed to design the site. Local figures joined the campaign, and soon the group made contacts with powerful figures in the Japanese government. People from Japan began to visit, often bringing small items to place on graves – a lock of hair, a flower. And as the gardens progressed Kibbler began another project – 2000 cherry trees that would link the cemetery to the garden. Kibbler and the group were sometimes reviled for his efforts: he and his family were on occasion abused by other locals who saw his efforts in a different light. But Don Kibbler's quiet efforts continued, and what was established is now an international shrine of gardens and memorials. In 1988, with the Gardens visited yearly by thousands of Japanese, he entered into discussions about another important Japanese grave – that of I-124.

Backed by a powerful Japanese sponsor, Kibbler toured Japan, speaking to the relatives and friends of the dead crew. The intensity of feeling generated by these people was impressive, he recalls, and he has some conjecture that this was to do with the Japanese Shinto religion, which asks that the bones of the dead will be returned to the land of their birth. At the Yasukini Shrine, where all Japanese war dead are honoured, he spoke to members of the Japanese Submariners' Association, including members of I-124's squadron, who together with family members, wanted the remains of the I-124 crew returned to the land of their birth. Influential members of business and government were met. Darwin RSL President "Lofty" Plane was also flown to Japan; he laid a wreath for Australian POWs at the Peace Park in Hiroshima, and seems to have been another part of the massive effort made by powerful Japanese sources to raise the submarine.

Kibbler was impressed by the support given to the proposal, and armed with promises of help, returned to Australia. He arranged to travel to the Northern Territory and consult with the NT Government. There, too, support was forthcoming. A site at Darwin's WWII gun emplacement fort of East Point, with a developing military museum taking shape, was picked out for the raised submarine. An organisation was formed to oversee the project: the NT/Japan Foundation. Letters of support from the Chief Minister, Marshall Perron, and Cabinet Minister Barry Coulter eventuated. The project looked set for success.

Meanwhile negotiations were continuing on the technical side of the project. Armed with specifications about lift points from Kawasaki, Kibbler was able to present a definite proposal to potential salvors. A heavy lift ship based in Singapore was considered to be the best means of raising the weight of the 80 metre submarine. The cost of the project in 1988 dollars would be in excess of $6 million.

With many such arrangements in place, the project finally hit a major obstacle. The Japanese federal government was unwilling to approach the Australian federal government and propose the raising; in the light of having requested protection for the submarine a decade earlier it would now seem a complete about-face. When Don Kibbler tried to approach the Hawke government of the day he says he was met with a lack of co-operation. Kibbler recalls that, despite the NT Government's written support and approaches through his local MP, his efforts were rejected. The project was abandoned in late 1989.

Further light is thrown upon the matter by the inspection of copies of correspondence between the Federal Department of Arts, Sport, the Environment, Tourism and Territories and McCarthy of the Western Australian Museum. McCarthy's own report on the submarine, completed in 1991, raises the possibility of raising the wreck too. However, the Federal Government's correspondence reveals it was against the raising because of the impact it would have on Japan. Writing after the *Flamingo Bay*'s voyage, the Federal Department said:

> ...the submarine constitutes a war grave. It is that fundamental principle which must drive all management options of the wreck site. Accordingly your recommendation to "decide on its long term future" and "to raise, conserve and display" is totally unacceptable to the Commonwealth Government. Such a purpose would also cause immense distress to the families of the submarines (sic) lost on the *I-124*.

Deloraine crewmembers in Darwin during 1992 for the 50th anniversary of the attack on Darwin. (l/r): Norm McKinnon, Stan Hale, Frank Marsh, Clarrie Rogan, Fred Savage, Ralph Mortimer, George Bryce. (Frank Marsh)

CHAPTER 15

– *I-124* TODAY

In what sort of condition is *I-124*; will she lie peacefully on the seabed, and what is her future? The questions will perhaps be of more importance as time passes. The submarine is significant in a historical sense: she is a link to WWI submarine design and engineering, and to the wartime conditions, equipment and methods of the Imperial Japanese Navy of World War II. However, in the harsh salt water conditions corrosion is a factor to be considered. How long will the wreck endure?

Some consideration needs to be given to the fact that *I-124* was a fighting submarine in a combat zone when she was sunk. As such, she was carrying torpedoes and mines, and many of these probably remain within the submarine's casing. While the Navy divers of 1984 examined the exterior of the boat thoroughly, it was not part of their brief to penetrate the submarine's interior, which – with the exception of an open hatchway that does not appear to lead anywhere – remains sealed up, despite Harry Baxter's claims. What of *I-124*'s war stores may be expected to remain inside the submarine?

I-124 certainly laid mines while she was in Northern Territory waters; according to the sources: 27 on 16 January. However, there is no record of any others being launched, and given the capacity of the submarine; at least 42 (or perhaps 48 according to Hashimoto), this might mean that 21 mines may still be on board the submarine. These may be expected to be within the stern mine room, waiting for release behind the mine doors. While these are not exactly a weak point, being heavily armoured and sealed, the doors were certainly designed to be opened, and as such are a weaker section than the overall pressure hull.

Whether there are any mines residing between the two hulls seems doubtful: the RAN inspection in 1984 was quite exhaustive, and specifically commanded to look for such objects. (Henri Bource's observations – he was the photographer during the Sub-Sea Services dives – set out in an interview with McCarthy, described drums: "in the shape of 44 gallon containers". These may very well be compressed air cylinders, the aircraft refueling tanks or ballast tanks).

In the forward hold we can expect a number of torpedoes; while it probably was the case that

12 were carried inside the submarine, we cannot be sure how many torpedoes remain. *I-124* may have fired more than one torpedo at *Deloraine*; she may have attacked other ships before her sinking. It would seem to be highly probable however, that some torpedoes are inside the submarine – it will be remembered that the *Curlew* dives found none stored between the hulls. Some of these may be within the bow tubes. If the outer cap corrodes, might these torpedoes be exposed to the outer sea and eventually be released? Perhaps not – a torpedo is a large and heavy object and it is not the case that one may arrive on the surface as a newly released mine not long exposed to water might be expected to do. However, it seems doubtless that large quantities of very dangerous explosives remain within the *I-124*'s hull – a container that is in very good condition, but which is suffering a little more corrosion each year.

Therefore it would seem to be sensible to implement a system of regular checks of the submarine to determine that there is no significant deterioration. McCarthy's opinions as to the hull's capacity for withstanding the ongoing effects of corrosion, made within his report, are worth considering:

> ...if the corrosion process is allowed to continue to the level of that noted on the WWII German submarine *U 853* where the relatively thin outer hull has begun disintegrating, consideration should be given, as was done in the case of *U 352* off the coast of North Carolina, to the presence of torpedoes and mines. In the *I-124* case, some of these munitions appear likely to have been stored within the outer and inner hulls...

> On *U 853* and on some other submarines of an older vintage, the thin outer hull has almost totally degenerated leaving the much stronger and thicker inner pressure hull exposed but otherwise intact...

> In general, by virtue of its shape and the strength of the pressure hull, an intact sunken and undisturbed submarine has the potential to provide a medium with which to preserve machinery, information and artifacts for examination in the future. There is however a point beyond which even the pressure hull will begin to break down....

> What appears to be extensive corrosion is evident on the upper deck casing.

There must also be the question of what is inside the submarine apart from explosives. Certainly a toxic atmosphere that would present pollution problems if it escaped – even if only a minor one. The *Flamingo Bay* voyage ROV report speculated on the nature of *I-124*'s interior:

> ...the question arises as to the likely environment existing within...Consideration

must be given to the likely effects of battery acid in liquid and or vapour form. Gases due to reaction of acid with seawater and other materials. Gases attributed to decomposition of organic matter (crew, food stores) taken into account.

In summary, there would seem to be a definite case for regular inspection of the submarine, primarily to ensure its continuing stability as a monument and a tomb, but also to safeguard against possible escaping dangerous munitions or pollution. The wreck has not, however, been visited significantly since the 1984 dives carried out by the Navy – the *Flamingo Bay* voyage inspection, while capably done, was too restricted to allow much detail to be ascertained.

And what of the submarine itself? It is now nearly 70 years since the sinking; Japan and Australia are significant trading partners and friendship exists between the two countries. The war is not forgotten, and nor is the significant role played by both sides. In February 1992 crew members of *HMAS Deloraine* traveled to Darwin to take part in the 50th commemoration of the attack on the city and its harbour in 1942. Frank Marsh, Clarrie Rogan, Norm McKinnon, Len Crabbe, Ralph Mortimer, Stan Hale, Fred Savage and George Brice all met in the city they had helped defend 50 years previously. The sinking of *I-124* was vividly remembered by them all – a quick and deadly action that very nearly saw the deaths of these men and their shipmates rather than the crew of the Japanese submarine. Every year the commemoration of the attacks on Darwin is held on the Esplanade, and it seems the history of the war in the Top End is growing in the country's collective consciousness. The submarine will not be forgotten either.

I-124 is an important shipwreck in excellent condition, not penetrated since its sinking, probably watertight except for some flooding, maybe at the stern. She is upright, with her gun and external hull still intact, and has some minor damage to the conning tower fairings. She carries her crew, their weapons and equipment, and is a snapshot of the Imperial Japanese Navy at war. While she still carries her war codebooks, she does not contain any other controversial cargo: not war loot, or secrets, or a cargo or ballast of mercury. However, she still contains her war stores, and she will not lie in her present state forever. She should be regularly inspected, and if items are found to have become dislodged, perhaps to be lost in the mud and sand below, then those artifacts should be recovered for posterity, preserved and displayed so that these submarine warriors and their fight are not forgotten.

Darwin City (Ken Hodge 2005)

Mitchell Street, Darwin (Bidgee 2007)

Darwin Skyline (Bidgee 2007)

Modern Darwin, capital of Australia's Northern Territory. The Territory is now a thriving part of Australia, with tourism, mining and defence as its three main employers. The Territory remembers its turbulent past regularly however, and is often visited by both veterans of WWII and Cyclone Tracy.

A fanciful picture of the minelaying squadron running on the surface with a smaller submarine in the foreground. This is reproduced from the front cover of the Japanese Maru magazine of some years back; Japanese interest in WWII has gone through a resurgence in recent years. Maru magazine, Japan

APPENDIX: *HMAS DELORAINE* – SHIPS COMPANY

SURNAME	GIVEN NAME	*PREFECTURE*	POSITION
Achison	Joseph (George)	SMN	
Ashworth	Sidney	SMN	
Atkins	Douglas	SMN	
Baxter	George	LS	Cook
Beaumont	Len		
Board	Sydney		Stoker
Bottcher	Maurice	SMN	
Brice	George		Signalman
Buckley	Aubrey	SMN	
Burke	Dan		Stoker
Collins	William (Tommy)		Stoker
Conlon	John		
Crabbe	Len (Buster)		Telegraphist
Crannage	Ken	LS	
Crawley	Alfred		
Crisp	Arthur	PO	Stoker
Ctercteko	William	ERA	ERA
Elmer	Jock	PO	ERA
Elwin	Robert		ASDIC
Fitzgerald	Henry		
Foggo	Robert		Stoker
Fraser	Douglas	LS	
Gartner	Reginald		
Gee	Charles		
Gibbons	R (Carol)	SMN	
Gilmoore	Tony (Doc)	SBA	
Gosper	Cyril		
Graham	Ken	LEUT	
Graham	Torrance		
Green	Tas (Terrip)	SMN	
Hale	Stan	AB	Electrician/wireman
Harvey	BJ	LEUT	ASDIC Officer
Healey	Harold	PO	Bosun/coxswain
Heywood			
Holder	Richard	SMN	
Hook	Arthur (Andy)	PO	
Hornery	William	LS	Telegraphist
Howard	Hedley	CPO	Chief Stoker
Howarth	Hilary		
Jackson	Gordon	LS	
Jones	Lindsay	SMN	

SURNAME	GIVEN NAME	PREFECTURE	POSITION
Just	Lance		Telegraphist
Kelly	Michael	PO	Supply
King	Edgar (Tom)	PO	
Langley	Alfred (Robert)	in hospital during the action	
Lindley	Adrian (Aub)	LS	Stoker
Marsh	Frank	SMN	Stoker
Mawer	Stephen	LS	Stoker
McDonald		ERA	
McKinnon	Norman	Signalman	
McSweeney	Bryan		
Meldrum	(Sandy) Alex	LEUT	1st Leut
Menlove	Desmond	Commanding Officer	
Millar	Robert		
Mollett	Arthur		
Moore	Lawrence (Pony)		
Mortimer	Ralph	ASDIC operator	
Northey	Jim (Jumbo)	Telegraphist	
O'Meara	James		Stoker
O'Neill	Harold (Peggy)	AB	
Owen	Frank		
Peters	Roy		Stoker
Pilcher	Jack (Boots)	Stoker	
Pitcher	Jack		
Popplewell	William	Stoker	
Rogan	Clarrie		Stoker
Ryan	Emmott		
Salway	Allan		
Savage	Frederick	LS	
Smith	Stanley (Wizard)		
Stevens	C		
Studeman	Dan		
Taite	Carson J	LS	ASDIC
Thompson	William Eric	LEUT	Gunnery Officer
Tindale	William		Stoker
Travers	Eric		Supply
Walker	William		Wireman
Waller	Arthur (Boysie)	PO	Stoker
Webster	Stanley	SMN	

AB=Able Seaman, ERA=Engine room artificer, LS=Leading Seaman (equiv.Army corporal), PO=Petty Officer, CPO=Chief Petty, SBLT=Sub-Lieutenant (equiv. Army 1st Lieutenant), LEUT=Lieutenant, LCDR=Lieutenant-Commander (equiv.Army major)

HMAS Deloraine - as at 20 Jan 1942, from Australian Archives: National Office, CRS A4624/1, List of Deloraine personnel, Penguin Tenders, Quarter ending 31 December 1941. Annotations to this from crewmembers Len Crabbe, Eric Thompson and Frank Marsh.

APPENDIX: *I-124* – SHIPS COMPANY

Surname	Given Name	*Prefecture*	Position
Kishigami	Koichi	*Kagawa*	Captain
Hisatoshi	Kouzo	*Kagawa*	Torpedo Chief Officer
Tajiri	Masao	*Nagasaki*	Navigator
Endo	Takao	*Aichi*	Division Commander
Abe	Takao	*Okayama*	First Lieutenant/Chief Medical Officer
Ishikawa	Bunzaburo	*Ibaragi*	First Lieutenant/Chief Engineer
Kotake	Ryou	*shikawa*	Sub Lieutenant
Watanabe	Tsunemi	*Kanagawa*	Second Sub Lieutenant Engineer
Watanabe	Nobushige	*Gunma*	Second Sub Lieutenant Engineer
Kawata	Yasushi	*Ibaragi*	Second Sub Lieutenant Engineer
Tojima	Chuji	*Akita*	Second Sub Lieutenant Engineer
Akiyama	Sensuke	*Tokyo*	Chief Petty Officer
Shimazawa	Shichitaro	*Tokyo*	Chief Petty Officer
Shimoda	Seizou	*Kanagawa*	Chief Petty Officer
Mansaku	Gunma		Chief Petty Officer
Koike	Katsuto	*Shizuoka*	Chief Petty Officer
Yagi	Touemon	*Shizuoka*	Chief Petty Officer
Tamura	Katsutaro	*Shizuoka*	Chief Petty Officer
Murakami	Yoshiaki	*Iwate*	Chief Petty Officer
Inoue	Torakazu	*Hokkaido*	Chief Petty Officer
Shiratori	Shigeo	*Aichi*	Chief Petty Officer
Zouga	Genpei	*Kanagawa*	Chief Petty Officer Engineer
Hoshino	Yukio	*Gunma*	Chief Petty Officer Engineer
Yamada	Hidekiyo	*Yamanashi*	Chief Petty Officer Engineer
Sasaki	Masayoshi	*Miyagi*	Chief Petty Officer Engineer
Kobayashi	Eiji	*Chiba*	Petty Officer Private First Class
Uchida	Shouhei	*Saitama*	Petty Officer Private First Class
Iwasaki	Otozaburou	*Ibaragi*	Petty Officer Private First Class
Ootomo	Hidenobu	*Ibaragi*	Petty Officer Private First Class
Ikeda	Sajirou	*Ibaragi*	Petty Officer Private First Class
Suzuki	Yoshio	*Shizuoka*	Petty Officer Private First Class
Suzuki	Aijirou	*Shizuoka*	Petty Officer Private First Class
Ikeda	Yorihisa	*Nagano*	Petty Officer Private First Class
Satoh	Tomiji	*Miyagi*	Petty Officer Private First Class
Satoh	Genshirou	*Akita*	Petty Officer Private First Class
Katoh	Masaru	*Hokkaido*	Petty Officer Private First Class
Okazaki	Masahisa	*Hokkaido*	Petty Officer Private First Class
Kanai	Haruo	*Gunma*	Chief Petty Officer Engineer Private First Class
Satoh	Fukuo	*Shizuoka*	Chief Petty Officer Engineer Private First Class
Saitoh	Mitsuo	*Fukushima*	Chief Petty Officer Engineer Private First Class
Ujiie	Mitsuo	*Iwate*	Chief Petty Officer Engineer Private First Class

Surname	Given Name	Prefecture	Position
Ishida	Kinichi	Yamaguchi	Chief Petty Officer Engineer Private First Class
Saitoh	Togo	Chiba	Petty Officer Paymaster Private First Class
Tominaga	Komao	Akita	Petty Officer Paymaster Private First Class
Kodaira	Kenichi	Nagano	Petty Officer Second Class
Tsunoda	Tatsurou	Nagano	Petty Officer Second Class
Takahashi	Kyushichi	Fukushima	Petty Officer Second Class
Abe	Houji	Miyagi	Petty Officer Second Class
Takahashi	Tomio	Iwate	Petty Officer Second Class
Iwamatsu	Kouji	Hokkaido	Petty Officer Second Class
Sakata	Sachiyo	Tokyo	Petty Officer Second Class
Ootaki	Riyouhei	Ibaragi	Petty Officer Second Class
Uchida	Teiji	Shizuoka	Petty Officer Second Class
Saisu	Toshinori	Fukushima	Petty Officer Second Class
Suzuki	Jinkichi	Akita	Petty Officer Second Class
Jinbo	Toyozou	Kanagawa	Petty Officer Third Class
Furuya	Torazou	Ibaragi	Petty Officer Third Class
Tabata	Takeo	Shizuoka	Petty Officer Third Class
Miyajima	Yasuyuki	Nagano	Petty Officer Third Class
Ishida	Minya	Fukushima	Petty Officer Third Class
Sasaki	Eisuke	Miyagi	Petty Officer Third Class
Kuwabara	Fukuo	Tokyo	Petty Officer Third Class Stoker
Nemoto	Kaoru	Chiba	Petty Officer Third Class Stoker
Sakata	Shichihei	Saitama	Petty Officer Third Class Stoker
Sasanuma	Matsujiro	Tochigi	Petty Officer Third Class Stoker
Kouda	Isao	Ibaragi	Petty Officer Third Class Stoker
Shimada	Teiji	Shizuoka	Petty Officer Third Class Stoker
Kawata	Tomizou	Nagano	Petty Officer Third Class Stoker
Komatsu	Sakuichi	Nagano	Petty Officer Third Class Stoker
Marushige	Hisayoshi	Nagano	Petty Officer Third Class Stoker
Maruyama	Hiroyoshi	Fukushima	Petty Officer Third Class Stoker
Murakami	Tomo	Miyagi	Petty Officer Third Class Stoker
Itou	Iwamatsu	Iwate	Petty Officer Third Class Stoker
Kawabata	Ishimatsu	Aomori	Petty Officer Third Class Stoker
Kobayashi	Masayoshi	Yamanashi	Petty Officer Third Class Medical Orderly
Kishimoto	Chuuzaburou	Yamanashi	Petty Officer Third Class Paymaster
Kousha	Isamu	Osaka	Petty Officer Third Class Paymaster
Warinou	Hideyoshi	Chiba	Seaman First Class
Kubota	Yukio	Shizuoka	Seaman First Class
Ogawa	Haruhide	Saitama	Stoker First Class

References

BOOKS

Alford, Bob. *Darwin's Air War*. NT: Aviation Historical Society of the NT, 1991.

Atkinson, James J. *By Skill and Valour*. Australia: Spink & Son, 1986.

Auphan, Rear Admiral Paul. *The French Navy in World War II*. Annapolis USA: United States Naval Institute, 1959.

Bishop, Chris (Ed.). *World Sea Power*. London: Temple Press, 1988.

Blair, Clay, Jr. *Silent Victory: the US Submarine War Against Japan*. New York: Bantam Books, 1975.

Boyd, Carl & Yoshida, Atihiko. *The Japanese Submarine Force and World War II*. Annapolis: Naval Institute Press, 1995.

Campbell, John. *Naval Weapons of World War Two*. Annapolis, USA: Naval Institute Press, 2007.

Carruthers, Steven L. *Australia Under Siege: Japanese Submarine Raiders*. 1942. Sydney: Solus Books, 1982.

Drea, Edward J. *MacArthur's Ultra: Codebreaking and the War against Japan*. 1942-1945, Lawrence, Kansas: University Press of Kansas, 1992.

Dull, Paul S. *A Battle History of the Imperial Japanese Navy*. Annapolis: United States Naval Institute, 1978.

Edmonds, Walter D. *They Fought With What They Had*. Boston: Little Brown, 1951.

Eldridge, F.B. *A History of the Royal Australian Naval College*. Melbourne: Georgian House, 1949.

Frame, Tom. *HMAS Sydney, Loss and Controversy*. Sydney: Hodder and Stoughton, 1993.

Friedman, Norman. *Submarine Design and Development*. London: Conway Maritime, 1984.

Gill, G. Hermon. *Royal Australian Navy 1939-1942*. Melbourne: Collins, 1957.

- - - . Royal Australian Navy 1942-1945. Melbourne: Collins, 1968.

Gillett, Ross. *Australian and New Zealand Warships 1914-1945*. NSW: Doubleday, 1983.

Griffiths, Owen. *Darwin Drama*. Sydney: Bloxham and Chambers, 1946.

Hashimoto, Mochitsura. *Sunk. The Story of the Japanese Submarine Fleet*. London: Cassell and Company, 1954.

Haultain, CTG. *Watch off Arnhem Land*. Sydney: Roebuck, 1971.

Holmes, WJ. *Double Edged Secrets*. Annapolis: Naval Institute Press, 1979.

- - - .   Undersea Victory. New York: Doubleday, 1966.

Ito, Masanori. *The End of the Imperial Japanese Navy*. London: Weidenfeld and Nicolson, 1956.

Jane's Fighting Ships of World War II. Studio Editions, 1990.

Jenkins, David. *Battle Surface*. Sydney: Random House, 1992.

Keatts, Henry & Farr, George. *Dive Into History*. New York: American Merchant Marine Museum Press, 1990.

Lewis, Tom. *Wrecks in Darwin Waters*. Sydney: Turton and Armstrong, 1992.

Lockwood, Douglas. *Australia's Pearl Harbour*. Melbourne: Cassell, 1966.

Lott, Arnold. S. *Most Dangerous Sea*. Annapolis: US Naval Institute, ???

Mackenzie, Vice Admiral Sir Hugh. *The Sword of Damocles*. United Kingdom: The Royal Navy Submarine Museum, 1995.

McDonnell, JE. *As You Were*. Publisher unknown, 1948. (Chapter copy in possession of the author)

Montgomery, Michael. *Who Sank the Sydney?* NSW: Cassell, 1981.

Mulholland, Jack. *Darwin Bombed*.

Nesdale, Iris. *The Corvettes*. self published, South Australia, 1982.

- - -. Small Ships at War. self-published, South Australia, 1993.

Norton, Frank. *Fighting Ships of Australia and New Zealand*. Sydney: Angus & Robertson, 1953.

Orita, Zenji. *I-Boat Captain*. California: Major Books, 1976. (trans: Harrington, Joseph D.)

Polmar, Norman and Carpenter, Dorr B. *Submarines of the Imperial Japanese Navy 1904-1945*. London: Convoy Maritime Press Ltd, 1986.

Potter, JD. *Admiral of the Pacific*. London: Heinemann, 1965.

Powell, Alan. *The Shadow's Edge*. Victoria: Melbourne University Press, 1988.

Preston, Anthony and Batchelor, John. *The First Submarines*. London: Octopus Books, 1975.

Rayner, Robert. *The Army and the Defence of Darwin Fortress*, NSW: Rudder Press, 1995.

Roscoe, Theodore. *United States Destroyer Operations in World War II*. Annapolis: United States Naval Institute, 1953.

Rossler, Eberhard. *U-Boat: the Evolution and Technical History of German Submarines*. London: Arms and Armour Press, 1981.

Rusbridger, James and Nave, Eric. *Betrayal at Pearl Harbor*. New York: Summit Books, 1991.

Stevens, David (Ed.) *The Royal Australian Navy in World War II*. St Leonards, NSW: Allen & Unwin, 1996.

Stevens, David. *Papers in Australian Maritime Affairs No.15, A Critical Vulnerability – The Impact of the submarine on Australia's Maritime Defence 1915-1954*. Commonwealth of Australia. Sea Power Centre–Australia. 2005

Studeman, Dan. *A Small War*. self-published, Pennant Hills, NSW, 1992.

Taylor, JRW. *Gold from the Sea*. Sydney: Australasian Publishing Co., 1943.

United States Navy. *Dictionary of American Naval Fighting Ships, Volume 1*. Washington, Navy Department, 1959.

USN Naval Historical Center. *Dictionary of American Naval Fighting Ships*, http://www.history.navy.mil/danfs/e2/edsall-i.htm, accessed 18/10/10.

US Naval Intelligence. *Uniforms and Insignia of the Navies of World War II*. London: Greenhill Books, 1944.

Wallace, Bob. *The Secret Battle*. Ringwood: Lamont, 1995.

Watts, Anthony J. *Japanese Warships of World War II*. New York: Doubleday, 1966.

Watts, AJ / Gordon, BG. *The Imperial Japanese Navy*. London, McDonald, 1971.

Wheeler, Keith. *War Under the Pacific*. Illinois: Time Life, 1980.

Williams, Captain Sir John. *So Ends this Day*. Melbourne: Globe Press, 1981.

Wilson, Michael. *Royal Australian Navy Profile No 2, Australian Submarines, Destroyers and Escorts*. Marrickville: Topmill, 1995.

Winslow, WG. *The Fleet the Gods Forgot – The Asiatic Fleet in WWII*. Maryland, USA: Naval Institute Press, 1982.

Winter, Barbara. *H.M.A.S. Sydney, Fact, Fantasy and Fraud*. Brisbane: Boolarong, 1984.

- - -. *The Intrigue Master*. Queensland: Boolarong, 1995.

FILMS

Maynard, Jeff. *Niagara's Gold*. Lindfield: Bacon Town Films, 1994.

DEFENCE DEPARTMENT

Department of Defence file 1/15/3, "Historic Shipwreck Japanese Submarine *I-124*". *HMAS Coonawarra*, Darwin, NT.

Gillett, Ross (Ed.). "Top End Navy", commemorative magazine, Waterloo, Percival Publishing, 1986. (courtesy *HMAS Coonwarra* Historical Collection)

AUSTRALIAN ARCHIVES

Australian Archives: Anti-submarine operations. Victorian section, Series no. MP1185/8/12. Item no. 1932/3/51.

Australian Archives: Operations against Enemy Submarines at Darwin by H.M.A. Ships *Katoomba*, *Lithgow* and *Deloraine* and U.S. Destroyers *Alden* and *Edsall* - 20/ 21 January, 1942. (Archival numbers not present on copy)

Australian Archives: Australian War Memorial, CRS A78, *HMAS Deloraine*, 1942.

Australian Archives: NSW, Series SP551/1, Bundle 330, Deck Log of *HMAS Kookaburra*, 18-30 January, 1942

Australian Archives: Australian War Memorial, AWM 124 4/16, Radio play: "Death of a Sub", by Peter Hemery, May 1942.

Australian Archives: National Office, CRS A4624/1, List of *Deloraine* personnel, *HMAS Penguin* Tenders, Quarter ending 31 December 1941.

Australian Archives: National Office, CRS A4624/1, List of *Kookaburra* personnel, *HMAS Melville* Ledger and Tenders, Quarter ending 31 December 1942.

Australian Archives: Admiralty 789 to ACNB re diving attempts, Victorian section, 28 and 30 January 1942. Series no. MP1185/8/12. Item no. 1932/3/51.

Australian Archives: N.B Four Five Four to NOIC Darwin re diving attempts, Victorian section, 28 January 1942. Series no. MP1185/8/12. Item no. 1932/3/51.

Australian Archives: signal to *Coonawarra* from ACH Darwin (?) re diving and second submarine, Victorian section, 23 January 1942. Series no. MP1185/8/12. Item no. 1932/3/51.

Australian Archives: D.N.O. Northern Territory to *Lithgow* and *Deloraine*, Victorian section, 23 January 1942. Series no. MP1185/8/12. Item no. 1932/3/51.

Australian Archives: A.C.N.B. to NOIC re contacting Capt Williams Victorian section, 31 January 1942. Series no. MP1185/8/12. Item no. 1932/3/51.

Australian Archives: D.N.O. Northern Territory to A.C.N.B. 473 re Captain Williams' readiness, Victorian section, 31 January 1942. Series no. MP1185/8/12. Item no. 1932/3/51.

Australian Archives: A.C.N.B. to D.N.O. N.T. 27 re Captain Williams' equipment, Victorian section, 1 February 1942. Series no. MP1185/8/12. Item no. 1932/3/51.

Australian Archives: NT Region, CA 1070 Administrator NT, CRS F425, Item C137 Pt 2; Report from Harbourmaster on Fujita Salvage voyage to Bathurst Island, 15 August, 1960.

OIC, HMA Anti-Submarine School, Operations against Submarines, 16 February, 1942. Series no. MP1185/8/12. Item no. 1932/3/51.

Australian Archives: section of *HMAS Melville* 1942 report, AWM 70, 400, courtesy Phil Franklin.

HMAS Melville War Diary; Australian War Memorial; Series Number AWM 78; Control symbol 400/2.

JAPANESE WRITTEN REPORTS AND SOURCES

Agawa, Hiroyuki. *The Reluctant Admiral: Yamamoto and the Imperial Navy*, (orig. published in Japan as *Yamamoto Isoruleu Shinchusha* in 1969), translated by John Bester, Kodansha, Tokyo, 1979.

Association for the Publishing of Japanese Navy Submarine History. *A History of the Imperial Japanese Navy Submarine*, Tokyo, 19??. (orig. published in Japan as *Nihon Kaigun Sensuikan Shi*); sections translated by Ms. Li Xiao, Darwin, 1995; Ms. Jodie Kell, Darwin, 1995-6; Mr Ken Yonemoto, Japan, 1995.

Japanese Embassy. Letter advising of crew numbers, 9 May 1995.

Office of the Chief of Military History, Japanese Monograph No. 102, "Submarine Operations December 1941-April 1942". Military History Section, Headquarters, Army Forces Far East.

Shibuya, Tatsuwaka. Map showing minelaying squadron sortie south - Jan/Feb 1942, in *First Stage Navy operations, Submarine Forces Record*, unpublished, 1957 - copy provided by Professor Teruaki Kawano from The National Institute for Defence Studies, Tokyo, Japan.

Imperial Japanese Navy. *List of Navy Officers*, Department of the Navy, Tokyo, 1940 and 1941 editions.

United States Naval Historical Research Centre, Washington Navy Yard, Washington, DC.

Evans, EE. Memorandum to Commanding Officer, *USS Trinity*, 20 Jan, 1942.

Gregory, JW. Commanding Officer *USS Holland*, Report to the Naval Officer in Command, Darwin, 31 Jan, 1942.

Gregory, JW. Commanding Officer *USS Holland*, Report to the Commander in Chief, Asiatic Fleet, 1 Feb, 1942.

Hawes, Rear Admiral Richard E. USN, Biography. (supplied by Louis Wiegand).

Pacific Strategic Intelligence Section. "Japanese Submarine Operations, 23 January to 25 March 1942". Commander in Chief United States Fleet (In possession of Barbara Winter)

Ships' Historical Section. "History of *USS Langley*" Department of Naval History, US Navy.

Snyder, Ralph W. "Statement made of 2/22/90 concerning whether *Holland* divers entered *I-124*". Handwritten witnessed statement.

USS Edsall. Commanding Officer's Report: "Activities of *USS Edsall* for January 20-21", 22 January, 1942.

USS Holland. "War Activities of the *USS Holland*". List of dive team personnel. Medical Officer's report - pp 6-7.

USS Trinity. US Naval Transportation Service, "War Diary".

USS Sailfish. Commanding Officer's note to CO of *USS Holland* on commendable performances of *USS Holland*'s divers, 6 June 1942. (In possession of Elmer Feltz)

Wilkes, J. First endorsement to CO *Holland* - secret letter, 6 February, 1942.

USS William B. Preston. Ship's Log extract, including hand-drawn map.

HANSARD EXTRACTS

Australian Senate. Historic Shipwrecks Bill, 1976. Second Reading - debate. p. 2333, 1 December 1976.

Australian Senate. Japanese Submarine: Mercury Contamination Risk. (Question No. 1882) p. 3068, Thursday, 28 May 1992.

FEDERAL POLICE FILES

Australian Government Solicitor. Letter to AFP, Darwin, 21 October, 1985.

Occurrences. "Diving on *I-124* submarine"; "Further enquiries in relation to *I-124*"; "Request for AFP assistance re I124". File 3/89, 15 March 1989.

Occurrences. "Request for AFP Presence at *Flamingo Bay*" File 3/89, 16 March 1989. (Includes handwritten undertaking signed by Mike McCarthy and David Tomlinson.)

McCormack & Associates. Lawyers acting for Hawks, Chadderton & Tyers, Letter, 26 April, 1973.

Statement. Peter John Collett, Lieutenant, RAN, 11 December 1984.

MAPS AND PLANS

Corvette plans. Drawn by David Rowland for *The Wooden Warship*, Sydney, 1995.

I-124 Blueprints. Kawasaki Heavy Industries, Tokyo, Japan. (Courtesy Don Kibbler). Graphic of *I-124* drawn from this by Jenny Crockford.

South-East Asian Map. Courtesy of Department of Asian Relations and Industry and the Trade Development Zone Authority, Darwin, NT, 1996.

ARTICLES

Button, James. "Act of Forgiveness", Story on Don Kibbler. *Time*, 8 June 1992, (65).

Dermoudy, Peter. "The I124: a Japanese Submarine Wreck in Clarence Strait". Occasional paper No. 34, State Library of the Northern Territory. Darwin, 1992.

Hancock, David. "The Secret of *I-124*", *People* magazine. May 1989.

- - -. "Jap Subs are Still Menacing Darwin", *The Australian*. 15 April 1989.

Hall, Bernard. "*Sydney* was sunk by torpedo in saving raiders." *Daily Express*, London, 1 December 1941. WA Maritime Museum, file MA-630/81.

Hornery, Bill. "*HMAS Deloraine* at Darwin 1941-1942." *HMAS Scuttlebutt* magazine, Ballina section: Naval Association of Australia, January 1992. (6-9).

Jenkins, David. "Did a Sub Really Fire the Fatal Torpedo." *Sydney Morning Herald*, 17 September 1992, (15).

Mainichi Newspaper. "*I-124* Submarine is Blown Up." 13 July, 1977. (In possession of CJ Hawks)

Mawbey, Vaughan. "The $2 million Graveyard!" *Australasian Post*. 12 March, 1981. 4-5.

McDonnell, JE. "The Corvette's Kill", in *As You Were 1948*. Canberra: Australian War Memorial, 1948.

NT News. "I'll sue - says Atkinson. Battle looms on the *Peary*." May 27 1960. (1)

- - -. "Secrets not sunk with this U-boat." 12 December 1972. (7).

- - -. "Mercury pollution fears over the submarine salvage." 7 March 1973. (6).

- - -. "Japanese sub a war grave?" 30 March 1973. (1).

- - -. Advertisement: "Scuba Diving School Opens." 6 April 1973. (10).

- - -. "Rich mercury claims on submarine doubted." 12 April 1973. (1).

- - -. "Hands off - Darwin diver warns Japanese. 23 April 1973. (1-2).

- - -. "Japanese complain of Govt. attitude to submarine." 24 April 1973. (7).

- - -. "Sub. site." 26 April 1973. (1).

- - -. "Navy acts to halt salvage work on sub." 26 April 1973. (3).

- - -. "Japanese rap diver over sub. salvage." 8 May 1973. (4)

- - -. "Submarine yours, Japan told." 20 June 1973. (2)

- - -. "Sub salvage bid to be filmed." article by Terry Hartney. 20 September 1976, (1).

- - -. "Leave sub alone, says Sinclair." 18 October 1976, (7).

- - -. "Diver 'must comply with regulations.'" 21 October 1976, (2).

- - -. "Boat found over sub wreck." 12 January 1984. (1-2).

- - -. "Reverse decision on sub." 15 March 1989, (4).

- - -. "Submarine claim 'garbage'." article by Julia Cooper. 17 March 1989, (5).

- - -. "The day we sank a sub off Darwin." Interview with *HMAS Shepparton* crewman Jack Valli, 10 June 1989, (19).

- - -. "Wreck dive off - Jap sub will be inviolable." 7 March 1989, (13).

- - -. "2nd sub found off Bathurst", article by Paul Jackson. 27 May 1989, (1).

- - -. "Mystery war sub was lump of rock" article by Genny O'Loughlin. 13 August 1989, (3).

Reinhardt, Denis. "Suspect motives in French attack on Aussie trawler." *The Bulletin* magazine, December 23, 1986, (56).

Souter, Gavin. "The Death of the Dreaded *I-124*", *The Sun*. 9 May, 1973. (10-11). (also published in the *Sydney Morning Herald*, April 21, 1973. (15))

Standard Newspaper. "Darwin bombing reunion." NSW, February 4, 1992. (8)

Sankei Newspaper, Japan. Article on attempted salvage and Historic Shipwrecks Act, 13 July, 1977. (In possession of CJ Hawks)

Stevens, DM. Lieutenant Commander, RAN. "The Sinking of *I-124*." *Australia's Navy 1992-93*, (78-81) - article supplied by David Stevens.

- - -. "The role of radio intelligence in the anti-submarine war around Australia, 1942-45." *Journal of the Australian War Memorial*. 25 October 1994. (22-30)

- - -. "The last Japanese submarine off Australia." *Journal of the Australian War Memorial*. 22. April 1993. (35-41)

- - -. "South-West Pacific Sea Frontiers". *The Royal Australian Navy in World War II*. St Leonards, NSW: Allen & Unwin, 1996.

Sun Newspaper. "Corvette Sank Submarine Twice Her Size." no byline, August 3, 1976. (20)

Williams, Denis. "The Sub with a Million Secrets." Sunday Press, *The Age*. 22 April 1984. (9).

Unsourced:

Article: "Honour for sub four decades later." Unidentified regional NSW newspaper, 1988. (In possession of Mrs Jean Menlove)

Article: "Sub Salvage." Unidentified newspaper. (In possession of North Australia Collection, NT Library)

Article: "Row brews over sunken mystery sub." Unidentified Victorian newspaper. 1 April, 1973. (In possession of CJ Hawks)

PLAYS, MONOGRAPHS, DIARIES, LETTERS

ABC. Document Archives - letter to the author, 25 May 1995.

Amemiya, Hiroshi. Japanese representative of CJ Hawks and partners, 1973. Letters. (In possession of CJ Hawks.)

ASIO. Letter to the author re arrest powers, 20 February 1995.

Baxter, Harry. Statement, signed, undated, biographical account of 1970s first salvage attempt in company with Chadderton, Hawks, and Tyers. (In possession of the author)

Bucknall, Ruary. Biographer of Sid Hawks: "Sid Hawks - Seafarer, Storekeeper and Adventurer", manuscript, 1995

Campbell, David. Commodore, RAN Naval Attache in Washington, USA, letter to Director, Japan Section, Department of Foreign Affairs and Trade, 28 December 1989.

Carpenter, Jon. Specialised on-site conservator. ROV report. One page report compiled on *Flamingo Bay* member, in NT Museum *I-124* file.

Chatterton, John. "History 1: Attempted Salvage of *I-124*" (In possession of CJ Hawks)

Crabbe, Len. Crewmember - *HMAS Deloraine*, letter to the author 25 July 1995.

Craike, William H. Commander (ret'd) RNZNR, crewmate of Desmond Menlove, letters to the author, November-December 1995.

Crane, RH. Commander, RAN, Dive Team Leader *HMAS Curlew*, letters to the author, 1994-95.

- - -. Commander, RAN, report on dive operations, from *HMAS Curlew* at sea, 3 December 1984, in Department of Defence file 1/15/3.

Dale, Harry. Able Seaman on board *HMAS Karangi*, Diary 1942, North Australia Collection, NT Library.

Drea, Edward. Author - *MacArthur's Ultra*, letter to the author, 14 Dec 1994.

Federal Department of The Arts, Sport, the Environment, Tourism and Territories, Letter from Les Neilson, Assistant Secretary, Cultural Heritage Branch, to Mike McCarthy of the Western Australian Museum re raising of *I-124*, 4 October 1990.

- - -. Minute: "Record of Meeting between DASETT and Japanese Embassy officials, 22 June 1989. From NT Museum *I-124* file.

Ferrier, Ed. Letters to The *Australian* and the *NT News*, 14/17 March, 1989.

Feltz, Elmer. Chief Master Diver in *USS Holland*, letter to the author, May 9 1995.

Garrick Gray & Co. Letter to Mr Ian Cran, acting for T&L Salvage, 30 Jan 1973, in possession of WA Maritime Museum.

Gibson, Ian. Commander, RAN, Report of Proceedings from on board *HMAS Assail*, 1972.

Hale, Stan. Crewmember - *HMAS Deloraine*, letters to the author December, 1995 - March 1996.

Hemery, Peter. Play: *Death of a Sub*, ABC Field Unit, Darwin, May 1942.

Hornery, Bill. Crewmember - *HMAS Deloraine*, letters to the author Feb-March 1995.

Japanese Embassy. Letters to CJ Hawks and partners, 1973. (In possession of CJ Hawks)

Japanese Embassy. Letter to author re details of 1950s records, 9 May 1995.

Johnstone, John E. "Wrecks was my Business", unpublished manuscript circa 1970, original held by Jeff Maynard.

- - -. "Diver's Yarns". unpublished manuscript circa 1970, original held by Jeff Maynard.

Kishigami, Atsuko. Letters 1995-6. (translator Takashi Shoji.)

Laffer, Gordon. Letter to Mike McCarthy, WA Maritime Museum, re conversation with Bob Williams, 25 October 1990.

Marsh, Frank. Crewmember - *HMAS Deloraine* - diary entries - February 1942.

- - -. Crewmember - *HMAS Deloraine*. Letters to the author 1990-1995.

May, Ken. Spitfire pilot who bombed *Don Isidro* in WWII, letters to the author, 1989-1990.

McCarthy, M. Departmental Report. "The *Flamingo Bay* Voyage including reports on Japanese Submarine *I 124*, The Iron Barque *Ann Millicent*, Indonesian Divers at Cartier Island, Inspection of a site thought to be the *SS Koombana*", Maritime Archaeology Department, WA Maritime Museum, Fremantle, WA, 1991.

- - -.Various letters to the author, telephone conversations, Internet messages re *I-124* , 1994-96.

- - -.Letter to Les Neilson, Assistant Secretary, Cultural Heritage Branch, Federal Department of Arts, Sport, the Environment, Tourism and Territories, re raising of *I-124*, 17 October 1990.

- - -.Wreck Inspection Journal, Department of Maritime Archaeology, in NT Museum *I-124* file.

McCormack & Co. Lawyers, letters to CJ Hawks and partners, 1973. (In possession of CJ Hawks)

McDonald, Max. "International Naval Research Organisation", letter to the *NT News*, 26 December 1990, (9).

Menlove, Desmond. Handwritten notes on *I-124* action, 19??, in the possession of Mrs Menlove.

Menlove, Jean. Letters to the author on Desmond Menlove's career, 1991, 1995.

Mortimer, Ralph. Crewmember - *HMAS Deloraine*, letter to the author 17 February 1995.

Museums and Art Galleries of the Northern Territory, letter from Director Colin Jack-Hinton withdrawing dive permission, 20 February 1989, letter in possession of David Tomlinson.

Nason Papers, Submarine *I-124* file, 3/89, Department of Maritime Archaeology WA Maritime Museum (copy NT Museum)

Netherlands Embassy. Letter on ship *Bantam*'s history and Dornier squadrons' movements, 12 February 1996.

NT Police. Letter concerning Harry Baxter/klaxon, 15 March 1995.

Parker, David. Ex-RN/RAN submariner, letters re submarine design, January-March 1996.

Paine, Thomas. Director, Submarine Warfare Library, California, USA, letter to Mike McCarthy, 3 April 1990.

Partington, R. Captain, RAN, Director of Naval Operations, Letter to the Secretary of Federal Department of Arts, Heritage and the Environment, 7 March 1985, in Department of Defence file 1/15/3.

Price, Colin C. Crewmember - *HMAS Katoomba*, letter written at sea 24 February 1942, letters December, 1995 to February 1996.

- - -. Manuscript: "A Tiffy's Odyssey: being the recollections of a Royal Australian Naval Artificer 1941-1961." December 1995.

Purves, Frederick, Rear Admiral (retd.) and RAN diver in Darwin, WWII. Letters and annexures, 15 March, May 5 1996. (Letters written by son Robert Purves with his observations also added)

Rogers, J.A. Leading Telegraphist on board *Lithgow*, diary extracts 1942, in the possession of Phil Franklin, Darwin.

Ross, John. Naval officer based in Darwin 1946-7, letter to the author, 28 December 1995.

Royal Australian Navy. Background articles about *Deloraine* Trophy, undated. (In possession of Mrs Menlove)

- - -. Statement of Lieutenant Commander Desmond Menlove's service, from Director of Naval Officers' Postings. (In possession of Mrs Menlove)

Stevens, David. Director of Naval Historical Studies, letter to the author on hydrophone performance, 14 February 1995; advice on the "second submarine" theory, 21 January, 1996; advice on German Pacific presence, 14 February 1996.

Sub-Sea Services. "Project: Submarine Hull Inspection." Report, 3 pages, 8 March 1973.

Thompson, Eric W. Gunnery Officer - *HMAS Deloraine*, letters to the author July-September 1995.

Tranter, Guy. ABC Assistant Archivist, Letters to the author re Peter Hemery's play Death of a Sub, plus copy of June 1942 letter from BH Molesworth of the ABC, May 1995.

USS Holland. "Welcome Aboard brochure", US Navy, no publishing date, courtesy present *USS Holland*.

Wallace, Bob. Crewmember - *HMAS Warrnambool* phone conversations; letters to the author Nov-Dec 1995, letters 1996.

Waller, Arthur. Crewmember - *HMAS Deloraine*, letters to the author 14 February and 29 March 1995.

Wiegand, Louis. Crewmember - *USS Holland*, letter to the author August 1995.

White, Homer. Crewmember - *USS Holland*, letters to the author, January/April 1995.

ORAL SOURCES

Allen, Warren. Diver, Telephone interview, 20 March 1995.

Baxter, Harry. Interviews, Darwin, 5 & 16 February 1995.

Campbell, David. Rear-Admiral, 1989 RAN Naval Attache in Washington, USA, telephone conversation, 2 March 1995.

Chadderton, Johnny. Interview, 13 January 1995.

Cole, Steve, Lieutenant. RAN Dive Team II leader; discussions on dive techniques, underwater salvage and submarine construction, 1995-6.

Crane, RH. Commander. RAN Dive Team Leader *HMAS Curlew*, telephone interviews, 18 August 1995, and 18 March 1996.

Craven, Bob. Federal Police Det. Sgt., telephone interview 21 February 1995, interview 28 February 1995.

Endo, Mikiharu. Interview 4 October 1995 - Tokyo, Japan. (interpreter Takashi Komura)

Gibson, Ian. Commander, RAN, Captain of *HMAS Assail* 1971, interview 5 August 1995. Conversations 1995-96.

Hawks, CJ (Sid). Telephone interviews Jul/Aug 1989, interviews August 1989, July 1991, September 1995, conversations 1989-96.

Kibbler, Don. Telephone conversations November 1984, interview - 14 January 1995, and personal conversations 1995.

Kilgariff, Bernie. Senator involved in Historic Shipwrecks Bill, telephone interview 17 September 1995.

Kishigami, Atsuko. Interview 1 October 1995 - Tanabe, Japan. (interpreter Takashi Shoji)

McCarthy, Mike. Curator - Western Australian Maritime Museum, conversations, 1995-96.

Marsh, Frank. Crewmember - *HMAS Deloraine*, conversations, Darwin, 1992.

Morris, Harold. Crewmember, *HMAS Kuru*, interviews, August, 1995.

Muller, Sasha. Master SCUBA Instructor, conversations on diving at depth and mixed gases, 1995-1996.

Nason, James E. Financier of Baxter *I-124* project, telephone interview, 14 January 1996.

Parker, David. Ex-RN/RAN submariner, telephone interview, 9 March 1996.

Perron, Marshal. Diver, interview, 14 March 1995.

Plane, Lofty. Darwin RSL President, telephone interview 27 October 1995.

Porter, Jim. Ex-Baxter diver, interview 19 May 1995, conversations 1995-6.

Tiernan, Barry. Head of NT Police Special Branch 1970s, telephone conversation re Baxter recovery of *I-124* souvenirs, 21 November 1995.

Tomlinson, David. Captain - Research Vessel *Flamingo Bay*, telephone interview 29 July 1995, plus email on relevant chapters, 1995.

Torisu, Kennosuke, Commodore (Ret.). Imperial Japanese Navy 1927-45, Chief of Staff, Sixth Fleet, interview 29 September 1995 - Tokyo, Japan. (interpreter Ken Yonemoto)

Tyers, George. Diver - conversations 1988-1994, telephone interviews 13/26 February 1995.

White, Homer. Crewmember - *USS Holland*, telephone interview 16 February 1995.

Whitehead, Ian. Chief Petty Officer at *HMAS Watson*, telephone conversation on *Deloraine* trophy, 14 November 1995.

Wiegand, Louis. Crewmember - *USS Holland*, telephone interview 19 February 1995.

Web sites not included above

Gull Force, 2/21st.Battalion Association's History http://www.gullforce.org.au/Battalion_History.html 8 September 2010.

Imperial Japanese Navy Page. http://www.combinedfleet.com/kaigun.htm. See Sensuikan! Operational histories of Japanese submarines in WWII, by Bob Hackett and Sander Kingsepp. 26 October 2010.

Northern Territory Government. Place names register. http://www.nt.gov.au/placenames/register/2007/documents/ JarvisRdHawksCt-Herbert.pdf 14 September 2010.

INDEX

I

J

K

L

M

N

V

W

Y

Z